Rituals and Relationships in the Valley of the Sun

The Ketengban of Irian Jaya

INTERNATIONAL MUSEUM OF CULTURES

Publication Number 30

Marilyn Gregerson and Joyce Sterner
Volume Editors

C. Henry Bradley
Series Editor

William R. Merrifield
General Editor
Academic Publications Coordinator

Rituals and Relationships in the Valley of the Sun

The Ketengban of Irian Jaya

Andrew Sims and Anne Sims

A Publication of
Cenderawasih University
Jayapura, Irian Jaya
and
International Museum of Cultures
Dallas, Texas
1992

Copyright © 1992 by the Summer Institute of Linguistics, Inc.

Library of Congress Catalog Card No. 92–61811

ISSN: 0–0895-9897

ISBN: 0–88312–271–5

Cover sketch and design by Hazel Shorey

Copies of this and other publications of the International Museum of Cultures may be obtained from:

International Museum of Cultures
7500 West Camp Wisdom Road
Dallas, Texas 75236

Contents

Foreword

This volume is the result of a workshop conducted in Irian Jaya by Marilyn Gregerson and Ken Gregerson in October and November of 1989. It is the second major publication in the Cenderawasih University (UNCEN) and Summer Institute of Linguistics (SIL) project that focuses upon anthropological studies of the people and cultures of Irian Jaya.

Cenderawasih University sees special publications such as this extremely important at this time in the development of the country of Indonesia, and specifically Irian Jaya. Many changes are taking place at an accelerated rate. It is crucial that the people of Irian Jaya know where they have come from and with this understanding plan appropriately for the future. As the University plans for the future, this information will help guide us in offering help to our people as they seek to adjust to the changes that will take place as our country, Indonesia, looks towards the future.

Through this publication we also hope to generate, as well as disseminate, relevant information to concerned public and private agencies regarding the cultural context within which developmental activities must be made to operate effectively in the province.

I would like to take this opportunity to express my appreciation to all those who have worked long and hard to make this anthropological volume possible. I am especially indebted for the consultant and editorial assistance of Ken Gregerson, Marilyn Gregerson, and Joyce Sterner. Thanks also are due to the Governor of Irian Jaya and his staff.

August Kafiar
Rector, Cenderawasih University

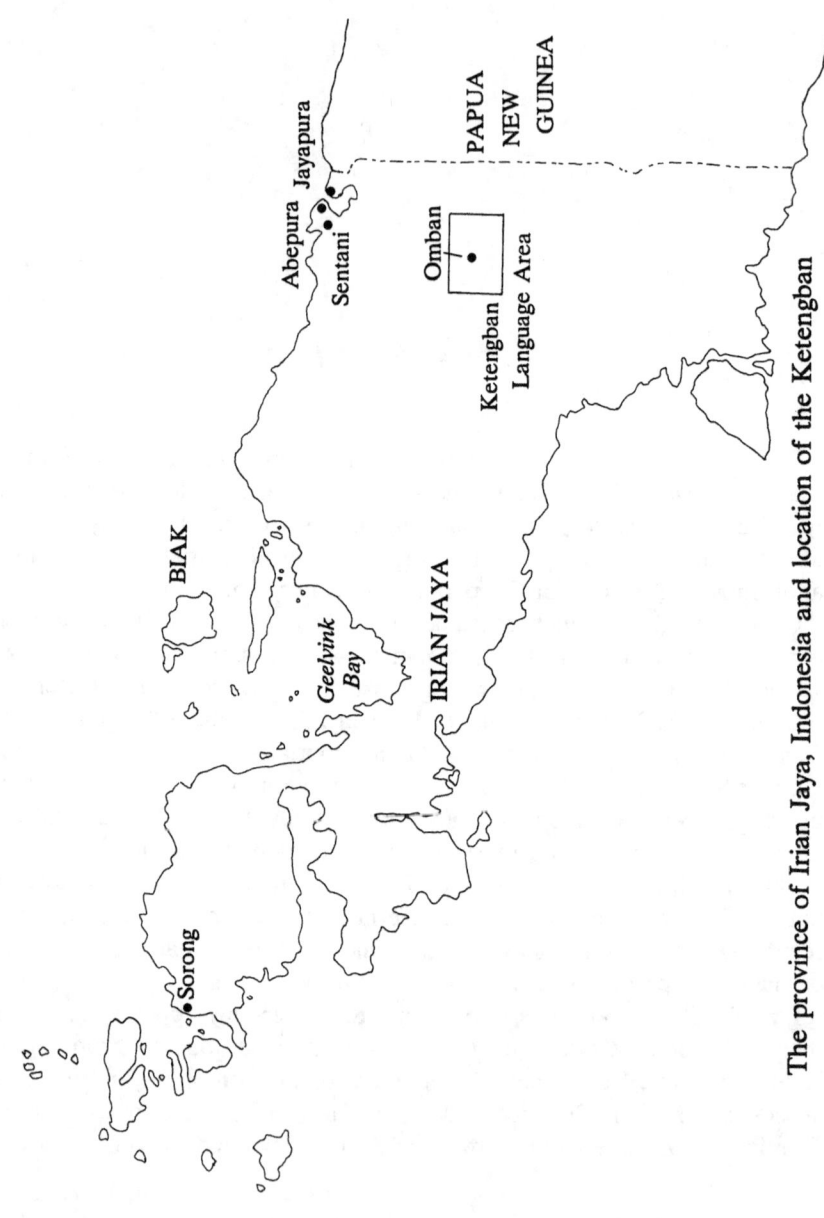

The province of Irian Jaya, Indonesia and location of the Ketengban

Preface

This second volume of anthropological studies of the people and cultures of Irian Jaya focuses on the Ketengban people who live in the eastern highlands of Irian Jaya, Indonesia in the District (Kabupaten) of Jayawijaya, subregency (Kecamatan) Okbibap.[1] The center of their territory is about one hundred twenty nautical miles due south of the coastal port of Jayapura and is bounded on the east by Apmisibil and on the west by Eipomek. They are scattered throughout a montane forest ranging in altitude from 2,000 feet to 6,500 feet in elevation and number between ten and twelve thousand people. They inhabit approximately eighty small hamlets scattered throughout the rugged mountains and live in small, round, walled, thatched houses built on pilings one to two meters above the ground. Traditionally these dwellings were clearly designated as either men's houses or women's houses. Though men's cult associations are still identifiable by membership in one of the larger men's houses, the strict restriction of men's versus women's dwellings have relaxed somewhat and family houses are more common now.

Contact between Ketengban and outsiders began in 1972. When airstrips were constructed to access this isolated area, eight to ten larger villages of 150 to 400 people formed near these links with the outside world. Today there is evidence of adaptation to the Indonesian culture, the Indonesian government, and Christianity. Large numbers of Ketengban have become adherents of Christianity, possibly as high as sixty to seventy percent of the population. If assessed by their physical culture and daily routines, most of

---

[1]For the earlier volume, see International Museum of Publications No. 17.

the more isolated Ketengban seem little influenced by the outside contacts. However, those living near the airstrips are seen using modern implements and clothing and making larger permanent gardens.

Like most highland peoples of Irian Jaya, the Ketengban are horticulturalists. The generally good soils and climate in the area reward their gardening efforts. Their staple food is sweet potato but they also plant taro, manioc, sugarcane, pandanus, bananas, and numerous green leafy vegetables. A number of more recently introduced food items do well in various parts of the area such as cabbage, tomatoes, lemon, jackfruit, papaya, maize, squash, cucumbers, onion, and several legumes. The Ketengban derive some animal protein from domestic pigs, and also from a very limited number of marsupials, birds, cassowaries, wild pigs, and wild dogs, for which they hunt in the forest using bow and arrow, deadfall, snare traps and dogs. Some protein also comes from snakes, lizards, tadpoles, frogs, and tiny fish caught along the numerous swift flowing streams of the area. Sago, though not unknown, is scarce and is not a primary item in their diet. Though all food may be exchanged, the most highly valued items in food exchanges are pork or other hunted game, pandanus, sweet potato, taro, and manioc.

The Ketengban are a patrilineal, patrilocal society. Kinship terminology distinguishes between cross and parallel kinsmen in the first ascending generation, ego's generation, and the first two descending generations. Terms extend bilaterally without distinguishing lineal and collateral kin.

The Ketengban language has been classified as Papuan stock and part of the Mek family in the Trans-New Guinea Phylum (Voorhoeve 1975 and Heeschen 1978:10). There are four dialect areas: the Central, Eastern, Western, and Northeastern, though all are mutually intelligible. Only the Northeastern dialect is markedly different in vocabulary and pronunciation.

My wife and I resided in the Ketengban area from 1981 to 1992 working in the Kerjasama program under the auspices of Cenderawasih University and the Summer Institute of Linguistics in analyzing and learning to speak the language of the Ketengban. The present volume of three papers is a compilation of material gathered from personal conversations with the people and from our own observations of their lifestyle. (Earlier versions of these papers appeared in *Irian,* published by Cenderawasih University.) We appreciate the help given by many of our Ketengban friends and language helpers. We are also grateful for the many hours of consultant and editorial help given by Marilyn Gregerson and Joyce Sterner.

Andrew Sims

Of Red Men and Rituals:
The Ketengban and the Supernatural

Andrew Sims

Contents

Cosmology

Aspects of the world view and traditional religion of the Ketengban people of Irian Jaya, Indonesia is the focus of the pages that follow.[1] Here I deal with Ketengban cosmology and their view of the nature and makeup of man, the spirit beings, both great and small who inhabit their world, and their ceremonial and ritual life as it demonstrates their attempts to live in harmony with their world.

Ketengban cosmology is holistic, not compartmentalized into physical aspects and spiritual aspects. The fact that the latter cannot be seen by ordinary men makes them no less real, powerful, and important; quite the contrary. The Ketengban live life as a physical and spiritual whole in constant dynamic interaction with their physical world and the beings who inhabit it. These beings include major and minor spirits who have lived in the world since its creation, the spirits of dead relatives and ancestors, and

[1]To complete this paper, an intensive time of inquiry and confirmation of data took place for approximately five months in 1989. The core group providing this material consisted of ten men and four women. Several of the men had been headmen responsible for various of the ceremonies in their areas and close kinsmen who had held such responsibility. All these men were past initiates in the *kwet* ceremonies and had either carried out or been present during the performance of the ceremonies described. Their ages ranged from thirty-three to fifty-five. The Eastern, Central, and Western dialect areas were represented in this group. Some material was gleaned from everyday occurrences, some from questions and probing, and some from lengthy unsolicited texts recorded during the period of study. I would like to express my appreciation specifically for the help of the following men: Musa Kulka, Andiokia Difur, Elias Basini, and Tomopnye Lefitalen.

the man or woman living in the next house or across the mountain pass in another valley. For the Ketengban man, woman, and child, life is neither secular nor sacred but comprised of a complex of different entities which must be dealt with.

At the present time Ketengban culture is in a period of transition. The main life ceremonies and major rituals reported herein have, from all appearances, been discontinued. However, it is difficult to determine the practices in many hamlets remote from contact with outsiders. In many ways the cosmology and world view of the people have not changed a great deal although Christianity has unquestionably had a significant impact on their beliefs. Many of the people no longer fear the spirits nor feel the need to placate and honor them. Due to the difficulties of speaking for the entire language group in understanding how much their view of the physical and spiritual universe has changed and the difficulties in trying to change tenses in the paper to be both accurate and coherent, this paper is written in the present tense. Use of the present tense in the section on Rituals may be misleading since all of these rituals are not actually in current practice.

The Ketengban people describe the universe as having at least four regions or layers. The uppermost level is the top of the sky (*im deike*), and almost nothing is known about it. The world that humans see and live in is believed to be a flat textured surface which is covered by a dome similar to an overturned bowl. This dome is not made of any describable material but is firm though somewhat fragile. The inner surface of the dome marks the upper limit of the sky. The top of the sky is above this dome. Everything found in the region between the dome and the surface of the ground is known as the middle sky (*im nitamai*). The mountains, valleys, rivers, and features of the earth's surface on which humans garden, travel, and live is the earth, land area (*tuai mutu*). The layer underneath the surface of the earth is known as the area under the earth (*tuai amutara*). There is no term for the lowest layer of the universe, which some Ketengban consider to be part of *tuai amutara*. However, all agree that this lowest layer exists and is the abode of the enormous spirit *bawa bo* (see figure 1).

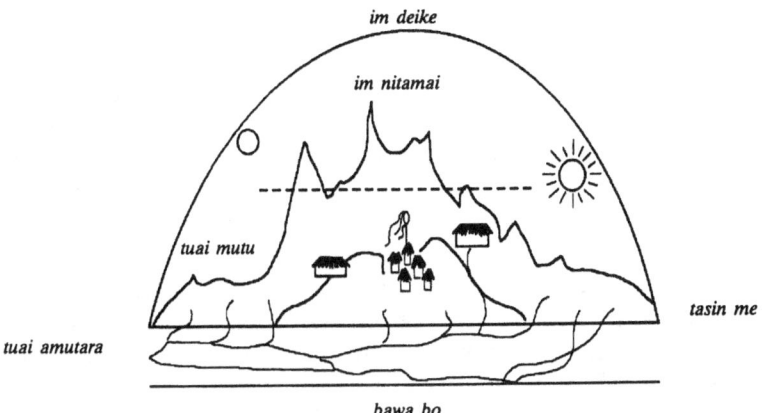

im deike

im nitamai

tuai mutu

tuai amutara

tasin me

bawa bo

Fig. 1. The Ketengban cosmos

Realm of the Sky Beings

In the first and highest layer (*im deike*), there live sky beings which have never had access to the human world nor is it possible for humans or spirits to visit their realm. It has no connection with great ancestors or spirits of past eras nor will spirits of the dead ascend to take up residence there in the future. The empirical evidence that sky beings live above the dome of the sky is that the root hairs of their sweet potato and taro plants are visible at night as they protrude through the "soil" so that the ends appear as stationary points of light, the stars. The sky beings are therefore known to be gardeners and, being aware of the humans in the world below their own, are considerate enough to use their dibble sticks with a softer sideways motion. If they use more force and a downward motion as humans do, they might "punch through" the dome of the sky and cause injury or death to humans below with the falling debris.

Realm of Man

Man lives in the realm between the sky dome and the area under the earth first in his bodily form and after death in his spirit form. Many Melanesians have been reported to be aware of and to interact regularly with a very large number of spirit beings (Habel 1979). This is also true of the Ketengban. In their view, most of this interaction takes place in the middle realm, further described in the section on The Spirits.

In this middle realm there are two distinct regions: the middle sky (*im nitamai*) and the earth (*tuai mutu*). The middle sky is the area just below the surface of the sky dome in which the sun and moon travel. They are living sibling spirits with the sun the sister and the moon her brother. During the day, the sun travels from the *keteng yakan tara* 'sun coming-from area' to the *keteng ban tara* 'sun going-to area'. The sun's daily journey begins beyond the river farthest east in the universe called *tasin me*, where the creator deity sent her in the beginning era. When she reaches the place where the sky dome and the earth's surface meet, the westernmost edge of the universe, she slips under the earth's surface and travels underground through *tu amutara* to the east and there awaits the return of her brother, the moon, and then begins her journey again. The northernmost and southernmost solstices of the sun signal the timing of the two most important cycle-of-life ceremonies of the Ketengban people (see the section on Rituals). Though less active in relation to men than many of the other spirits, the sun is thought to be very dangerous but her brother, the moon, is relatively unimportant.

Just like humans, both the sun and the moon have a body (*nonge*) and an essence (*deiyo*). What humans see traveling through the firmament as the sun and moon are the bodies of these beings. Their essence resides under the floor of the most important ceremonial house in Ketengban territory (*bopgon ati* 'Bopgon house'). A key ancestor, Wengep Lepitalen, was the headman of this house and he alone could see with spiritual eyes through the floor into the glowing essence of the sun and moon and predict weather patterns. He did not have any controlling power over them, but was the guardian of that spirit house. Secret names for the sun and moon are known to initiates of the male cult and can never be spoken openly, especially before women, noninitiates, or children, who do not understand their true nature. These secret names are *tasinpurupuru ner/keteng* 'the spirit woman coming from Tasin (Me)' and *ongopgenepe* 'the (moon) halo'.

The middle sky is also the area in which certain birds fly, clouds produce rain, rainbows appear, and certain types of spirits and spirit specialists travel from place to place. In the early mornings, just as dawn breaks, people can observe stars (*kwiri*) twinkling or in Ketengban terms 'quivering'. Their light is responsible for the milky way, (*kwiri tel* 'star light' or 'shining'). These *kwiri*, few in number, are different from the plentiful tuber root hairs of the sky beings described above. Though not active in human affairs, the *kwiri* are spirits which at dawn fall into streams, rivers, and ponds and in daylight are visible as tadpoles and small fish. Women and noninitiates, not realizing their true nature, regularly eat them, but since it is done in ignorance of the altered state of the spirits, no harm results. Initiated males who know their secrets have to say certain incantations before eating these tadpoles, yet for reasons connected with the potential for loss of personal power usually do not eat them.

Few features of the physical world are without spiritual significance to the Ketengban. The rainbow is thought to be spiritually significant and is one totem of the Wisal clan. It can be a sign of either good or impending doom depending on where it is pointing or resting. If it is overhead or pointing to a house or hamlet, it is called *nimi mi tu* 'the flesh of a child or person'. If seen over an unpopulated area of jungle, it is called *bal mi tu* 'the flesh of a snake's offspring'. The meanings associated with the colors and the interpretations of the presence of the rainbow are a prime example of the overlapping and interacting of the realms of men and spirits.

If the rainbow is seen near a village, it is a sign that someone (probably from that village) is going to be killed. It can also mean that people are on their way to do this killing. However, if the hamlet is one in which there are many Wisal clansmen (whose *lyouna* 'totem spirit' is the rainbow), it means that they have been feasting and the spirit is now leaving, happily fed and honored. If the rainbow is seen over uninhabited jungle, it is a sign that either there is a place where snakes have just been killed by people, or a place where there are snakes to hunt. Four primary colors in rainbows, recognized by the Ketengban, have names assigned to them reflecting these beliefs. Red is called *nimi mi yapye* 'blood of a person/child'; yellow is *nimi lin kun* 'a bit of human urine'; green is *mitu* 'gall' or 'bile sack'; and blue or purple is *ambupka,* the name of a deep purple tree seed, perhaps consumed by the snake or person.[2] All of these colors are related to things encountered inside the body of an animal or person and also in the body of a spirit, since they are similar to people.

Clouds are called *im ketna* 'sky smoke' and though their origin is unknown, they temporarily cover the clean sky, much like dirt, smoke, or "sleep matter" in people's eyes.

At the top of the earth (*tuai mutu*) where humans travel or hunt is the particularly dangerous area of the mountain tops, highest ridgelines, and

---

[2]Adjusting the main noun from person to snake makes the name specific for village or jungle location, i.e., *bal mi yapye* 'blood of a snake'.

the largest and most spectacular waterfalls where specific spirits (*parum*) reside (see the section on The Spirits). The lowest part of man's realm is the earth's surface including the mountains, streams, rivers, valleys, flora, and fauna. It could also be described as the arena where the drama of life is played out by men and minor spirits. Here men are born, build homes, take wives, garden, raise livestock, and have children. Men receive signs or encounter spirits of various kinds from the physical features and fauna of their world. Certain animals, reptiles, insects, or birds may be the embodiment of spirits or their helpers and messengers. Massive rocks, trees, waterfalls, and certain locations are the habitation of spirits.

When a person dies his spirit may take the form of several kinds of birds. One of these, the *deman* bird, can give a whole range of signals to the informed man. A long low whistle indicates someone will die; a warbling call which sounds "wet" means that the spirit's mouth is full of blood and people are coming to kill the kinsmen of the man hearing the call. Other distinctive calls could mean that a war party is approaching, friendly visitors are coming, someone elsewhere has died, or his jungle marsupial trap has captured an animal.

Encountering (and foolishly killing) a white field mouse or a certain marsupial, *belep*, in the daytime could mean that the spirit it embodied would send many "children" to destroy crops throughout the area by pest infestation. If many flies landed on a person's skin, it could mean that someone was committing incest in the area, angering the spirits, and lead to massive crop failure from rot. Unexplained perspiration when starting a cooking fire in the men's house could signal the onset of a crop failure. There are many other ways the spirits interact with men in their realm as manifested by flora, fauna, weather, natural disasters, and physical features of the land itself.

In this realm of middle sky and earth the spirits of the dead continue interacting and participating for good and evil in daily life. It is also the stage where the drama of interacting with, appeasing, and honoring the major spirits of the Ketengban world is played out in rituals.

Realm of the Major Spirits

The next lower layer of the universe is the area under the earth (*tu amutara*). It is mainly characterized as the area through which the major spirits often travel. In this shadowy region there is a vast system of tunnels made from hollow trees (the most common tunnel-like formation found in the Ketengban world). The major spirits travel freely and instantaneously via these conduits to any area they choose. Some of the specific trees forming such tunnels are *gogopu, turuku, kono, teplem,* and *wause* which have hollow centers or are soft-wood trees whose centers quickly rot after falling. There are important "terminals" or holes in the ground functioning as access doors to the realm of man. These are at designated locations of key ceremonial or ritual houses throughout Ketengban territory but are visible only to certain spirit specialists. Through these underground passages and terminals the most important, powerful, and malevolent spirits gain access to the realm of men.

During initiations into the male cult these major spirits come out of the holes and participate in the rituals, dancing, and feasting. At other times they come out of similar holes to find people whose spirits are "ripe" for eating and so cause their deaths. These major spirits can also take people's spirits down into these holes resulting in their death. Hollow trees and bamboo in the jungle are extensions of the underground holes for the travel of spirits, but only some of them are visible to ordinary people. For example, the spirits can travel through hollow bamboo above ground and are able to make it bend over to touch the body or the roof top of a "ripe" or sickly person. By doing so they gain access to the body and the opportunity to eat the spirit, causing sickness and eventual death.

The lowest level of the universe is sometimes undistinguished from the level just described, but most Ketengban differentiate between them. From the beginning of time a deity has been sleeping in this lowest level under the entire earth's surface, or at least under the entire Ketengban territory. This deity is Bawa Bo and how he came to be sleeping there is described in the section on The Spirits. The essential fact for the Ketengban is that he must never be disturbed, and above all must never be awakened. Until recently, saying his name aloud or digging too deeply (such as when planting) was believed to invite disaster by waking him. When Bawa Bo twitches or slightly moves in his sleep, there is an earth tremor. When he is disturbed and shifts position a little, there is a major earthquake. Should he ever be angered or awakened and turn over or move significantly from his slumbering position, all of the earth's surface would be turned upside down and all living things destroyed. In 1976 there was a very destructive earthquake in the region where life began according to the Ketengban. Many people died, gardens and villages were destroyed, and international relief efforts resulted. Ketengban say that this was the night that Bawa Bo, upset by large numbers of Ketengban turning to Christianity, shifted in his sleep.

In summary, the Ketengban cosmology is multilayered, but visualized as a flat solid surface covered with the geographical relief of the earth, over which is the dome of the sky, like an overturned bowl. Above the bowl are the sky beings, below the sky dome down to the earth's surface is the realm of man, composed of three subregions: the middle sky where the sun and moon travel, birds fly, and various meterological phenomenon take place; the area of the highest mountain peaks and ridges, large waterfalls, and rock faces where certain semiretired spirits live and few men dare to go; and the surface of the earth where man interacts with his physical and spiritual environment, whether as a living being or an ancestral spirit. This is the abode of the minor spirits and where man communicates most intensely and intimately with the major spirits in his ceremonial and ritual life. Here also are the major spirits' entrances into the realm of man.

The underground layer is the abode and preferred area of travel for the major controlling spirits, characterized by a tunnel system giving access to all areas of the earth by doors which lead from this layer into the world of men. The lowest layer is the sleeping place of Bawa Bo, who could destroy all things by earthquake if awakened.

Mankind

The diagram in figure 2 represents a human being as conceptualized by the Ketengban, i.e., as a tripartite being composed of a body (*nonge*); a soul, spirit (*sambala*); and a heart, mind (*kange dipru*).

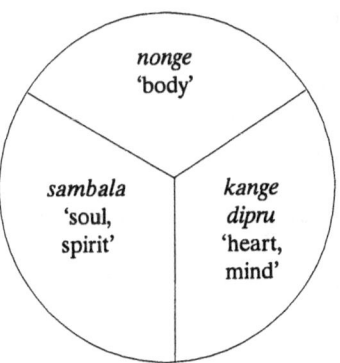

Fig. 2. Diagram of man.

The Body (*nonge*)

The body is that which is able to be seen, touched, and smelled. On the surface or inside the body, man experiences physical pain and sickness. Because a person's physical health and prowess affect his daily life, the Ketengban are attuned to bodily functions and sensations. However, the

11

Ketengban who have lived most of their lives without modern medicine appear stoic and unconcerned, even with painful and debilitating injuries.

Through the slaughtering of both wild and domestic animals, the Ketengban are familiar with internal organs and have names for each of the human organs, but have less knowledge of how they function.

Blood is considered a very important component and its loss (either visibly from injury or invisibly by becoming less strong or powerful) is a serious matter recognized as contributing to weakness and death. Blood is thought to be held in a reservoir in the chest and stomach area but also travels around in the veins. Bodily swellings, especially in the abdomen, are thought to be from the pooling of blood and are often precursors of death. Breath is an important indicator of life, and the lack of it is a symptom of death although people may be described as dead before the cessation of breathing. Pulse is not widely recognized as a life indicator for the Ketengban.

An intangible feature of bodies is that they may be hot (*buppe*), hard, strong (*gate*), cold (*bule*), or soft, weak (*boune*). To maintain a safe and productive life, especially during ceremonies, rituals, and warfare it is best to be hot and hard and avoid being cold and soft. Consequently, men should not eat tadpoles which might make them cold and soft unless certain incantations are said over them. This idea is due, first of all, to the belief that fallen stars take the form of tadpoles in the daytime, and also because tadpoles are of the cold and wet, weak and soft class of foods (i.e., tadpoles, frogs, and fish) which reduce man's power and make him more vulnerable. Water, also, should not be drunk for a certain period before, during, and after ceremonial events and rituals. There is a binary opposition here reminiscent of Lévi-Strauss' (1963) analysis of culture wherein men, heat, dryness, hardness, and power are desirable but diametrically opposed to and weakened by women, cold, wetness, and softness.

There are specific ways to attain hot or cold bodily states. Heat is enhanced by avoiding women, foods other than pork with blood in them, any reptiles, and water. There are certain times when it is desirable for a person to be made cold and wet in order to be unattractive to spirits who might otherwise come to "eat" them. A cold state can be enhanced at such times by a person being sprinkled with water and having certain incantations said over him.

Though physical features are less important to the Ketengban than strength, character, and interpersonal relationships, they do distinguish various body types, note differences in skin color or tone, and comment that some people are especially attractive. However, the body and its appearance is of less importance to them than to the average Westerner. Though a quick rinse to cool off or remove heavy mud is common, many Ketengban from the more isolated areas may go for months without washing or bathing. (Since prohibitions against water for men are in effect only for certain rituals, they are not a factor in matters of cleanliness.) On the other hand, the Ketengban are seriously concerned by the danger of being spiritually polluted or having one's power diminished by various associations. Eating taboo food causes problems because of the spiritual transgression of breaking rules, thus angering the spirits. The focus of Ketengban taboos is the damage to the spirit/soul and personal power.

Probably the most widely encountered example of spiritual pollution via physical contact in Melanesia is men being contaminated, either directly or indirectly, by menstrual blood (Lawrence 1965). For the Ketengban, such contamination is the worst imaginable thing that can happen to a man, resulting in widespread catastrophic calamity.

Another such physical pollution is possible after a death. The bodies of the deceased are traditionally put up in trees, or on high platforms, although on occasion they might be put in a garden or jungle house. In decomposition the body liquids drip onto the ground and anything nearby. If some excretion from the relative's corpse is even inadvertently consumed with food, a person is said to have *er apke beta dyepke* 'truly eaten his relative', so no one is allowed to eat anything grown near the burial area of a close relative. If any relatives of the deceased eat food items growing near the trees, house, or in garden plots nearby, the effects may be a swelling body and face, forgetfulness, ineffective work, mental confusion, an inability to perceive and avoid danger, and even death. Nonrelatives may eat such food about a year after the death.

Though there might be some physical precipitating event or catalyst, for the Ketengban the root causes of physical problems and sickness are spiritual. Except for warfare, sickness and death are caused by spirits. Therefore, Ketengban treatments have to do with the spiritual part of man, his relationships with people, and with the spirits.

Soul, Spirit Essence (*sambala*)

Every person has a soul or spirit which exists before birth. There is no concern as to the origin of the soul since it is received just as physical limbs are. It resides in the heart (*dipru* or *talema*) and is distinct from physical organs or their functions. The soul of a person is one's true essence and does not die with the physical body but leaves the body and continues living with the essential personality and characteristics of the person intact. The soul does not exit the body from any specified orifice but through the skin except for its final departure in the form of a fire-fly.

A person can experience soul loss or weakening through the actions of autonomous spirits in the Ketengban world or through the action of spirits of the dead. This state can be precipitated by numerous causes and agents, including breaking taboos, maintaining poor relationships with either people or spirits, action by sorcerers or other spirit specialists, and independent spirit or human malevolence.

The souls of shamans can travel through the air instantly to other places. Certain very powerful spirit specialists can "soul-travel" and their bodies also make the journey. They are invisible to the average person who cannot see a soul either when traveling or after death at which point it is called *nimi isok* 'person's evil spirit'. A person's soul may be stolen, eventually resulting in death. One common cause of a soul being stolen is by passing behind a fellow clansman. From time to time anyone may have the clan companion spirit (*kamaya*) sitting on the back of his neck or shoulders. This spirit becomes angered by a fellow clansman passing behind him. He then steals the offender's soul causing him to become insane and eventually die. Sometimes passing in front of someone or laughing without explanation in another's presence can have the same result. After the soul is stolen and taken away into the jungle, it gradually "matures" causing the person to get thin and weak and eventually die.

The soul can also have its essence "eaten" by various spirits. In some cases such stolen or damaged souls are recoverable, not through the victim's actions, but through the influence, skill, and power of the specialist called to help and the relatives intervening on his behalf.[3]

If a person does not die from calamity or sickness, but lives until he has white hair, no teeth, and wrinkled skin, and eventually dies in his sleep or while sitting in his house holding onto the poles around the firepit, he is said to have been a very good person. The soul of a person such as this (of which there are very few indeed) simply "flies away like a bird." When

---

[3]The souls of living people do not form relationships or any kind of alliances with the spirits of deceased persons or with other autonomous spirits. Therefore, though one's offensive behavior may result in an attack on one's spirit, one cannot in any direct way develop an advantageous relationship between other spirit beings and one's own spirit.

a person dies, the soul does not immediately leave the body to depart to some land of the dead but remains in the body or nearby the house or hamlet for several days until the body is placed in a tree. When the soul departs after death, it becomes the person's evil spirit and is then greatly feared. The spirits of the dead continue to live and be active in the world for a long time. They may be enticed to help man but are generally malevolent. The dead people (*deneng*), as they are also known, have a favorite habitation near the highest mountain peaks and ridgetops. However, they are so busy that they spend little time there.

Heart and Mind (*kange dipru*)

The third component of man recognized by Ketengban people is a complex called the *kange dipru* 'thoughts and heart'. The two facets of this complex are the heart (*dipru*) and the thoughts and mind (*kange tenena* or *kange*) which constitute a single concept in the perceptions of the Ketengban.

The heart is where a person feels positive emotions such as love, pity, and kindness. Negative emotions are sometimes described as being elsewhere in the body or as acting autonomously on the person. For instance, one way of describing intense anger is to say *mundu kupnere* 'my stomach has got me'. Another is *yu kupnere* 'anger has got me'. One seemingly negative emotion which does occur in the heart is *ne dipru nitam engenmane* 'I am crying in my heart'. This expression describes the kind of sadness engendered by the death of a close friend or relative, or a great disappointment.

The mind is the cognitive part of man with which he decides, forms opinions, makes plans, learns, and reasons. The thoughts and heart as a completed complex is not present at birth, as evidenced by infantile behavior, but somehow develops during the first twelve to eighteen months of life. A baby is not fully a person until the personality and mental processes are evident in its responsiveness and behavior. When this point is reached, the child is described as *kange konum deipmare* 'he has now placed his thoughts' meaning that his mental faculties are clearly present, and a reasonable degree of responsiveness and learning can be expected. Significantly, but perhaps also related to high infant mortality, children are not given names or treated as special until they become twelve to eighteen months old.

The term *kange* is applied similarly to adults. If someone does something stupid or which no one would normally have allowed, they might be scolded with the invective *kange mendeipmarem di do* 'is it because you do not yet have thoughts'. The implication which makes the rebuke more insulting is that one is still mentally an infant. More positively, when discussing what an absent person's response might be to a given situation, people say *er kange dia* 'from his mind' or 'whatever he decides he will do'.

The mind gives a person the ability to think, reason, and act in a responsible way. When it is adversely affected such as through drinking alcohol, it is said that the mind is lost or confused and tangled, thus accounting for a person's unreasonableness or irrational behavior. A similar confusing of the mind can be effected by spirits as mentioned above. It is reasonable then that for the Ketengban, the point of physical death is when there is no longer any speech or responsiveness to others. Unconscious or comatose people are categorized as dead even though they may still be breathing and have warmth and pulse.

These two facets of the complex heart and mind have been discussed separately to highlight their distinctives, but the Ketengban describe the two as one and sometimes use the words almost interchangeably, even though there are distinguishing nuances for this center of man's emotions and will.[4]

Origins, Totems, and Clan Founders

Ketengban mythology includes accounts of the assignment of totems to each clan and the way each clan was founded. The following is a summary of part of this mythology.

In the primordial era after the creator deity *doyap* had made the world, he assigned some of the major spirits to be helping and guardian spirits for each clan. Most of the animals, birds, and reptiles he created were ordinary, but certain spirits were given power to take the form of these creatures in order to be the clan totems. These spirit totems existed prior to the presence of human beings since, though the Ketengban do not describe it directly in this way, all people descended from these totem

---

[4]It is interesting that with the entrance of Christianity the Ketengban, on their own initiative, speak of the experience of believing Christ and the teachings of the gospel as taking place in the *kange dipru,* but that the Holy Spirit resides not in the *kange* 'thoughts, mind' but in the *dipru* 'heart'.

creatures. The general phrases used to talk about this topic supports this conclusion as in *nimi kwemdina deiyo* or *nimi deiyo keca* 'the basis of the creation of man (things)'.

Doyap assigned a totem (*lyouna*) to each predestined clan and sent it to certain Ketengban geographical areas. The Payumka clan has the cassowary (*sanipe*) totem and the associated spirit is *cangka ner*. The Uruwan clan has the python totem (*seremnye bal*) and its spirit is *ketlingna ner*. Certain clans have more than one totem and it is not clear whether the spirit took on more than one animal form or whether a multiple spirit connection exists. For instance, the Dipur clan has both a specific snake totem (*kitokke bal*) and a lorikeet totem (*wirye ma*). More commonly two or more clans share a totem though the implications for their initial descent are unclear. The Kipka, Payumka, and Mul clans all claim the cassowary as their totem and the Basini and Kulka claim the pig. Figure 3, though not exhaustive, lists some clan totems and spirits.

After going to the areas assigned by Doyap, the spirit totems usually had two offspring, a male and a female of their same kind, e.g., snakes and birds hatched from eggs, and marsupials from live births. These first two offspring then turned into humans almost instantaneously and soon "married" other totems and had children. The sons of the totems became the clan progenitors, providing the link with the totem for all future descendants.

For instance, if the totem was a snake, the male offspring became a man, took a wife from some other totem's female offspring, and their children were of the snake totem. The female offspring of the snake totem would be taken as a wife by the male child of another totem, and all their children would be of that male's totem, not their mother's totem.

Each human clan member has a special relationship with the spirit associated with his or her totem and can expect to receive from it help in healing, garden prosperity, and war. This help is usually mediated by specialists as described later, although anyone of a given clan can entreat their totem spirit. If a particular sickness or calamity is thought to be caused by one of these spirits, then a senior man of that totem's clan must remedy the situation by virtue of his special relationship with that spirit. The Ketengban say this relationship is analogous to a man and his dog or a woman and her pig. Just as these animals respond best to their owners, so totem spirits will not answer people not in their clan.

Region	Clan	Totem	Spirit
Bidoman	Lepitalen	*wirye* 'bird'	Kain Dyen Ngop
	*Lepye	*wirye* 'bird'	Kain Dyen Ngop
	*Muldam	*wirye* 'bird'	Kain Dyen Ngop
	*Malo	*wirye* 'bird'	Kain Dyen Ngop
	Dipur	*kitokke* 'snake' and *wirye* 'bird'	Ketlingna Ner
	*Wisal	*kase* 'bat'	Ketlingna Ner
	*Uruwan	*seremnye* 'python'	Ketlingna Ner
	Meiku	*wayu dyena* 'cuscus'	Ketlingna Ner
	Lepi	*kam* 'dog'	Ketlingna Ner
	Monggon	*wayu dyena* 'cuscus'	Ketlingna Ner
Basinduman	Kulka	*bisam* 'pig'	Memeduman Ngop
	*Bamme	*bisam* 'pig'	Memeduman Ngop
	*Deiyal	*bisam* 'pig'	Memeduman Ngop
	Mitne	*lyei* 'bird, crown pigeon'	Memeduman Ngop
	Kwace	*bisam* 'pig'	Memeduman Ngop
	*Keyan	*bisam* 'pig'	Memeduman Ngop
	Megouke	*wayu dyena* 'cuscus'	Memeduman Ngop
	Payumka	*sanip* 'cassowary'	Cangka Ner
	Kipka	*sanip* 'cassowary'	Cangka Ner
	Mul	*sanip* 'cassowary'	Cangka Ner

An asterisk (*) indicates that the clan is a subclan of the one above it.

Fig. 3. Clan origins, totems, and spirits

The following are two typical accounts of clan origins taken from my recorded texts.

The Dipur clan totem, *kitokke bal* '(a species of) snake', went to his assigned mountain and crawled into the hole under a *ba* tree to lay eggs, as observed by a Megouke clan woman. The snake eggs hatched and most were male. The Megouke woman came to see where the snake had gone into the hole and found it was actually a cave. She went inside and found the snakes writhing about. She was terrified as they encircled her but they turned into men, one of whom seduced her. She later bore children who were the ancestors of the Dipur clan. The spirit connected with this snake totem (Dipur clan) has the names *arambasisa ner* or *aramkiyap*, derived from the mountain (*aram*), the snake's name (*kitokke* or *kiyal*), the name of the *ba* tree, and the word designating either real (*sisa*), or spirit being (*yap*).

The Wisal clan's story is similar. The Wisal totem is the bat (*kase ma*) which went to a big cliff with a spring at its base. There the bat had male and female offspring, which became human. The offspring of the union of the Wisal man and a female of another totem are the Wisal clan. For the Kulka clan, Doyap sent a spirit in pig's form to a place called Mukupe where he wanted a spirit house built to be called *mukup ati* 'Mukup house'. The pig had several offspring. Some became men and one took a Wisal woman as his wife, and their offspring are the Kulka clan. The associated spirit was *mukupawenga* 'the one who went into Mukup house'.

An example of the accomplishments and contributions of these clan founders is the introduction of fire.

Long ago when Doyap was still on his mountaintop dwelling, Limgonai, a fire burned around him encircling the top of the mountain. After the creation and distribution of all things and the birth of the clan founders, Doyap was afraid that this fire would burn downwards and consume everything. So he collected the essence of this fire and gave it to a Dipur woman, who put the fire into some slow-burning tinder and stuffed it into her large hollow bamboo ear ornament. She carried this precious fire in her ear ornament for some time, causing her Kipka clan friend to rebuke her for being insensitive to the plight of all the people who did not have fire, who were cold and miserable and eating raw food. This criticism angered the Dipur woman and, removing the ear ornament containing the fire, she threw it disgustedly onto the ground. A nearby Kipka man saw the fire which had spilled out of the ear ornament, quickly snatched it up, and being a more considerate person, proceeded to share it throughout the area.

And so by this means fire came to the Ketengban, and this first fire has several well-known names which all include a reference to the place of origin (*limgonai*), to fire (*oukke*) (central dialect), and to the circumstances.

The names are: *limbarip oukke* 'fire encircling Lim mountain', *limkwerep oukke* 'fire which came down from Lim mountain', *limmap oukke* 'the fire which stayed/slept up on Lim mountain', *limbelek oukke* 'the long line of burning fire on Lim mountain'.

Man and Authority: Hierarchy of Power

The authority structure of the Ketengban people as prescribed by their traditional religion is shown in figure 4. Those at the top wield greater influence and power than those under them. The diagram does not include persons with political influence but only the power hierarchy specific to spirit beliefs.

Ritual Specialists	*asuru kwa neng*	shamans, those truly possessed
	mem deiyo neng	men responsible to carry out rituals
	kwetena neng	healers
	kerdona neng	sorcerers
Initiates	*kwet neng*	any initiated man
Noninitiates	*noupit neng*	uninitiated adolescent boys
	wisi nerepe	old women, some who assisted or knew something about ritual
	nerepe	women
	nyape	children

Fig. 4. Ketengban power hierarchy

The Ketengban do not believe that all men (and women) are created equal. The men of clans whose founders had good relationships and interaction with the spirits and deities in the primordial era are inherently more powerful than others. In some cases, this is because they were assigned responsibility for the ceremonies critical to the continuity or restoration and preservation of life and the social order. Other men are chosen by the principal power spirit, *kain dyen ngop*, to be shamans and ritual specialists. Some others, because of their relationships, their intelligence, or their good memories, are able to aspire to positions of relative spiritual power. But most men are not powerful in themselves or because they have great skill but only because of their kinship relations. Women are at the bottom of the scale of power and influence, although men occasionally show signs of fear of latent female power.

The following sections describe the major types of Ketengban spiritual authorities.

Shamans, Diviners

The most spiritually powerful Ketengban men are the shamans (*asuru kwa neng* 'men with branched eyes'). This name refers to the fact that these men have special relationships with the spirits which allow them to see and experience things which normal human beings cannot. These men have been chosen by the head of all malevolent spirits, Kain Dyen Ngop, to be spirit mediators, and he controls the hearts and lives of these men. Kain Dyen Ngop is thought to be the spirit of Um Bo. No other spirits ever possess men. These shamans are given "spiritual eyes" to see things in the spiritual realm and are active as diviners, healers, and helpers, but conversely are feared more than any other human beings because they are so powerful. They lead lives like the major spirits; they are active in killing, traveling invisibly and instantly through Ketengban territory to do evil deeds; they are unstable and unpredictable and they make people uncomfortable in their presence, even while conferring power by association on those in good relationship with them. They are at the same time highly respected and greatly feared.

When men are arbitrarily chosen to be shamans by the principal power spirit, Kain Dyen Ngop, it becomes obvious to everyone. At certain times these shamans become increasingly active, and then those destined to become mediators are identified. Whenever Kain Dyen Ngop begins to dance (unseen), all the shamans also begin to dance throughout the land. At such times others present in the houses begin speaking in ecstatic languages, but those who begin to dance and shake are showing themselves destined to be shamans. After such dancing, the shamans can suddenly disappear, leaving the houses through the firepits (even if a fire was burning), through cracks in the floor or ceiling, or simply by going out the doorway. Although they are then not seen for awhile, they can be heard in the sounds of scraping on the roof tops, whistlings, or rustlings in banana trees or dead trees. All the other men in the men's house become very frightened, seize their valuables, run to nearby houses, and bar the doors to avoid contact with the shamans.

When the established shamans perform the *sangsemna* dance and disappear, some of the new mediators disappear with them, which indicates they have begun their new role. The activities and powers of the shamans cannot be taught nor are there apprentices, but the powers are given directly by Kain Dyen Ngop all at once. The timing of the granting of these powers or the onset of a period of shamanistic activity is unpredictable.

In their altered state, the shamans can see the spirits and accompany them anywhere in the land immediately and invisibly. Normal people can see them disappear or be present when they suddenly reappear after an absence. During that absence they might be seen in many different places, such as high in treetops, on mountain tops, or in other inaccessible places.

On some of these journeys the shamans are transported by Kain Dyen Ngop in order to serve him by killing someone in a different area. Often this is done by shooting people with special spirit arrows (*isok mare*) supplied by Kain Dyen Ngop. Sometimes this death by arrow is instantaneous, sometimes prolonged and painful, but it is initiated by Kain Dyen Ngop or the major spirits, not by the shamans.

Sometimes the shamans function as messengers for Kain Dyen Ngop. If sorcery has been performed by a specialist (such as killing many people in a particular hamlet), Kain Dyen Ngop sends the mediator of the affected area as a messenger. He suddenly appears in a house of the victims' relatives and falls unconscious. Those present search his person and the immediate vicinity of the house for evidence which would tell where the responsibility lay for the recent deaths. The sign is usually a leaf from a particular type of tree or palm from which bows are made. The palm is from a distinctive (usually distant) area and is usually in the shaman's hand or on the ground by the house. This sign shows that people or spirits from the area where those trees or palms are found are responsible. If from a northern area, the sign would be *deir* leaves; if southern, *wen* leaves; from the east, *sinim* leaves (those responsible are the *sinim bo cangne neng* or *yale tara neng* 'those shaping bows from *sinim* trees' or 'the people from the Yale area'); from the west the leaf is *uyar* and the people are called *uyar cangne neng* 'those shaping bows from *uyar* tree'.

If, however, the killers are from a nearby area, the shaman who arrives will shake all over and dance by bouncing rapidly and singing the *sang mut* song in which the area responsible is named. Though retaliation for sorcery is expected, the ultimate responsibility rests on those who are killed because they did not give proper respect and gifts to the spirits.

The shamans also sometimes function as *lap pena neng* 'diviners' or 'explaining people', although other initiated men can also fill this function. These diviners enable people to learn which persons or spirits are responsible for a sickness or death. After inspecting the person and the illness, they can determine what kind of spirit is involved and where it can be found to make an appeasing sacrifice. For instance, large facial swellings accompanied by diarrhea are usually attributed to the spirit *nunupkor ner,* and gifts can be taken to a certain high waterfall to appease her. In some cases, the shaman might advise calling a man of a particular clan to perform a ritual specific to that clan due to its relationship to that spirit.

Another function of the shamans is related to their office as explainers (*lap pena neng*). In this capacity, they report to people whether the major spirits (or the *tau pena* 'house spirit') are happy with their sacrifices. Men have to set aside vegetable foods, pork, and tobacco and place it on a shelf across from the door of the men's house to honor the great spirit Um Bo, but the immediate recipient is the spirit, Tau Pena, who resides on the shelf. The spirits come and take the essence of the food gift but since they prefer to travel widely to watch everyone they are often not present. Nevertheless, the gifts are obligatory, and usually within three to five days the Tau Pena spirits do come to eat the food. Normal people cannot tell whether the spirits are pleased with the sacrifice or whether further gifts are necessary. The shaman inspects the food on the shelf to determine whether the spirits have eaten its essence and are satisfied. If not, they say, "No, they (the spirits) have turned their backs on you, so more pigs must be given." The shaman can also report to the spirits when someone has not made gifts to them.

Another helpful function of the shamans is to locate and return stolen souls (*sambala*) to their owners' bodies before they become weak and die. The spirits of the dead (*nimi isok*) sometimes steal people's souls and hide them in the jungle. The shaman can, if entreated, ask the major spirits or Kain Dyen Ngop where the souls are hidden, go and bring them back and, with a ritual, reinsert the soul into the person. If they accidentally happen on a stolen soul hidden in the jungle, they can return it if they are so inclined. If one shaman steals a person's soul and is taking it away, another shaman, if quickly asked, might catch up with him and convince him to give it back.

The shaman can also reverse certain kinds of sorcery. This is most effective if the sorcery has been initiated and performed by a human as opposed to a spirit. The shaman can be told by the major spirits or Kain

Dyen Ngop where to find the small bundles of "leavings" used in sorcery. Upon retrieving them and performing a ritual, they will cause the first sorcery to fail. A similar intervention can stop sorcery by a shaman from a different area. Although the shamans do not fight one another, they sometimes argue or negotiate to gain a reprieve for someone. For instance, if a shaman shoots someone with a spirit arrow (*isok mare*) from Kain Dyen Ngop, takes blood from the victim, travels to a place where spirits live, and eats the blood, the person will surely die. However, if another shaman can be induced to go and intervene before the blood eating takes place, a ritual can be performed by him to restore health to the dying person.

Another type of healing performed by the shaman is to "pull out" certain spirits which are eating a person's heart or to grasp and remove the spirit arrows shot into them by spirits.

The shamans can also use their influence to protect people by driving away the ancestral spirits of another group during warfare. These ancestral spirits assist their living relatives in fighting, but the shamans can only temporarily succeed in ritually driving them away since such spirits cannot be killed and will return on another occasion.

If a shaman has been instructed by Kain Dyen Ngop to kill his own relative whom he really likes, he might refuse to carry out the directive. This act could result in his being punished by death but more likely by other means. For example, Kain Dyen Ngop or the spirits might take the disobedient shaman on their travels, but leave him stranded high in a tree, on a mountain peak, a house top, a rock, or some other difficult place. Kain Dyen Ngop might choose to hit him on the head with a rock or piece of wood, resulting in a deep sleep which may last for several days. The shaman is aware of the punishment upon waking.

Ritual Specialists

Ritual specialists known as *mem deiyo neng* were given responsibility by Um Bo for carrying out the major ceremonies and rituals of Ketengban life. Um Bo assigned certain ceremonies and rituals to designated clans and the ritual specialists are in charge of them. The ritual specialists are not spirit mediators like the shamans (*asuru kwa neng*) but are responsible to determine the correct time or season to hold the rituals, to insure that rituals are correctly performed, and also to determine whether a ceremony needs to be performed again. Having assigned people to begin preparations for the ceremonies, the ritual specialists have to insure that everything is done in accordance with the instructions given by the deity Um Bo in the beginning, because they are scrutinized by his spirit Kain Dyen Ngop. Their activities are discussed in the section on Rituals.

The responsibilities for the ceremonies, rituals, and incantations assigned to specific clans are passed within the clans to each new generation. Those ceremonies and activities appropriate to Lepitalen clansmen, for example, can be learned only by Lepitalen men, and no other clan can be successful in doing them. Every ritual or ceremony is intended to accomplish certain things related to specific causes, problems, or needs which are the special jurisdiction of specific spirits and, further, none can be successful without the help of the principal power spirit Kain Dyen Ngop. Each clan has to deal with the totem spirits and companion spirits with whom they have relationships and cannot influence the companion spirit (*kamaya*) or totem (*lyouna*) of other clans or groups.

The only exception to this are firstborn sons, who are considered related to their mother's clan's companion spirit and privileged to learn the ceremonies in her clan's domain. Good relationships with these men are desired because they can be called upon in situations needing ceremonies or rituals from either their father's or their mother's clan.

The ritual specialists choose their firstborn sons as apprentices, and this role cannot be declined or resisted. The firstborn sons are taught the incantations, songs, rituals, and ceremonies of their father's clan and are called elders (*du neng*).

Younger sons are generally not taught these things, but a back-up system is allowed. When the second (but no other) son is initiated, he can be taught some of the rituals and incantations by his father or by his older brother. This is insurance against the loss of this crucial knowledge should the father and eldest son die before the eldest son has a son old enough to be initiated. This secondborn son of the original father is allowed to practice the incantations and rituals and to teach the firstborn son of his older brother when he comes of age.

Healers and Sorcerers

These two categories of practitioners, the healers (*nimi kwetena neng*) and the sorcerers (*nimi kerdon neng*), though having different goals, nevertheless have relatively equal power and influence. In fact, some people are able to use their spiritual powers to heal in some instances and to cause sickness and death in others.[5] In either case, the sources of their powers are the same spirits discussed throughout this paper. Here they are grouped together since the focus is on their relative power and influence among the Ketengban. Healers are appreciated and respected. Sorcerers, while deemed necessary to punish wrongdoing, exert pressure, or get revenge, are more feared than respected.

One marked difference between these two types of specialists is that sorcerers, unlike any other class of spirit specialists, can be women. Such women are very old, the sisters of ritual specialists, and are the most feared sorcerers because their power is great and they are characterized as capricious, mean, and evil. Perhaps this fear is greater because this is the one area where women can exert power over men.

Sorcerers and healers are specialists associated with individual clans and spirits and are very dependable in times of need. It is essential, however, to determine which of them has the necessary connections for any given problem, and shamans and ritual specialists may be called on to make that determination if it is not obvious because of their clan membership. They can also deal with spirits with whom they have relationships, whether the clan totem spirits, the companion spirits, or the ancestral spirits. But shamans are notoriously unpredictable and may do harm rather than good. Given a certain problem, a person usually solicits a shaman's services merely to divine what person or spirit is responsible and then selects a sorcerer or healer from the clan most likely to succeed in getting revenge or solving the problem based on his relationship to, or knowledge of, the spirits and rituals in question.

The skills for healing and for cursing people are not necessarily handed down through filial lines. Other people can be taught the appropriate incantations (*merya pena*) and rituals. Specialists may select their apprentices, or a person may ask a specialist to take them as an apprentice. Apparently, women cannot make such a request or teach these things to other men, though they may occasionally teach other old women some specific things.

The second category in figure 4, *kwet neng*, refers to any man not a specialist in ceremonial or ritual life, unversed in incantations for healing or cursing, but who has been initiated into the male pandanas cult.

---

[5]There is frequent overlap among the categories of spirit specialists. Some shamans (*asuru kwa neng*) can heal; some ritual specialists (*mem deiyo neng*) can both heal and curse; and some men who are neither shamans nor ritual specialists have power to heal or curse or both.

Membership in the cult gives him the privilege of participating in all the major ceremonies, feasts, and rituals and opens the door for advancement into a more powerful category. Membership also gives the right to eat important ritual foods like pandanas and certain cuts of pork and generally to get greater amounts of pork and other food at feasts. Members of the cult or the men's round house are associated with important people, privy to knowledge, conversations, and discussions related to the spiritual and ceremonial life of the community, and also form the network of mutually beneficial obligations so important to life in Melanesia. Simply being able to participate in these things gives status above the last four categories on the chart.

A noninitiate (*nofet neng*), is considered less than a full adult. He is usually prepubescent and cannot associate with initiated men during ceremonial or ritual periods, which puts him in a class with women and other things which relate to spiritual weakness and pollution.

Since initiations are held approximately every three to five years, it is possible to be in the early teens and still be uninitiated. Competition and jealousy arise when some young men close in age are full members of the male cult and others are not. In order to avoid these feelings, there is a "halfway" arrangement worked out during the initiation. If men know that their young male kinsmen are not quite old enough to participate in the initiation rites, they can still gain some privileges for them. Just before the regular initiation candidates are taken to the secret enclosure, these younger boys are formally "introduced" to the ceremonial specialists and the candidates. One of their initiated kinsmen, usually an elder (*du ngop*) or a ceremonial specialist (*mem ngop*), puts the boy into a large net bag and hangs it around his neck. With the boy suspended on his body, the kinsman enters the men's house at the first stage of initiation and hands the child to one of the ceremonial headmen (*mem deiyo ngop*). The headman takes the net bag with the child and holds it out in front of him, walking around the circle of candidates and former initiates, displaying the boy to them while saying certain incantations. Then the boy is handed back to his male relative and sent home again, not participating further in the initiation. This procedure only procures for him the right to eat some otherwise taboo foods until he can be fully initiated. The most important of these foods is pandanas (*kain*) which is, except for pork, the most important social and ritual food for the Ketengban. This is no small privilege because, for most Melanesians as well as the Ketengban, feasting is not just an opportunity to consume a great deal of food but is an important time of cementing alliances, incurring mutual obligations, honoring the ancestors, and venerating the spirits. This introduction does not give these boys the right to be present at ceremonies, or rituals, or to hear about taboo subjects but does move them higher up the scale of power and importance than women and other things which pollute.

Finally there are the Ketengban women, who have the least power and influence with the exception of the old women sorcerers. Women have very few rights and privileges and no socially recognized avenues of power. Their normal workload is extremely heavy and never finished. Even today, when many of men's former responsibilities such as warfare and ceremonial life are no longer practiced, gardens and pig-raising still are the responsibility of women. It is common to see men sitting talking or taking a nap almost any time of the day. When a man goes to the gardens, he likely returns with only a small net bag of food, just enough to contribute to the evening meal in his men's house. Women, on the other hand, almost never rest or relax during the day but depart very early for the gardens, are gone almost all day, and return heavily loaded with three or four large net bags of tubers, greens, and firewood, often with a child on top and a pig behind on a rope.

Many of the most nutritious and ceremonially important foods were, but are not now, strictly taboo to women. Even to look at some of these foods, like pork back fat or inner stomach fat, certain taboo cuscus (marsupials), or red pandanas, can result in death at the hands of initiated men. To be seen anywhere near the main ceremonial locations is to incur suspicion of having seen men in their taboo red paint, ending in a quick brutal death with the body thrown into a cave or down a hole.

Small girls can be promised as wives well before puberty and neither they nor their female relatives are allowed to have a part in the decisions regarding these arrangements. Women are considered to be the primary and most dangerous source of spiritual pollution via their menstrual blood, augmented by the fact that they eat so many cold, wet, and weak foods like frogs, tadpoles, insects, small birds, and lizards.

Ketengban women are, however, very important to the men, though little privilege results from this worth. Women raise pigs and children, care for and harvest gardens, and the benefit of this work is acknowledged in the large bride prices paid for them. A man and his male kinsmen gain wealth through pigs, large gardens, and bride price, all of which contribute to his ability to enter an expanding network of mutually beneficial obligations.

Without the labor of his wife or wives and close female relatives, a man's potential in developing these alliances is severely hampered.

In spite of their general powerlessness, there are at least two ways in which women can deal very significant, devastating blows to men. The first way is, tragically, suicide. Such women often take a nursing child along and usually kill themselves by throwing themselves off a high cliff or into a raging river. In view of the extremely limited options open to them, it is clear why suicide is attractive and effective. In one blow, the husband loses his wife, chief gardener and pig raiser, his investment in future female children through whom to gain bride price, a possible son and heir, and incurs much trouble. He will still probably have to pay some if not all of the bride price, have strained relations or even fights on account of her death with his wife's clansmen, have to get his gardens and pigs taken care of through other female relatives, and might soon incur further debts and potential trouble in arranging for a new wife. This is no small blow, and even the threat of a wife committing suicide is a serious concern for men.

The second way a woman can exert power and create trouble for her husband, or the group in general, is by inviting the attentions of other men, especially men of other clans or areas. In this way, the wife causes tensions and the expenditure of time, effort, and even goods in settling such a problem. Her husband may be killed in the resulting fray, or the woman may lose her life, but these possibilities do not seem to be much of a deterrent. Sometimes sorcerers of either sex put curses on a woman to cause her to behave seductively and thus cause trouble for someone. There are specific rituals to prevent this irresponsible behavior. A further means of dealing a significant blow to a difficult or unresponsive husband is infanticide.[6]

In summary, there are no rigid castes or classes among the Ketengban, but there is a hierarchy of power and authority among men and women related to spiritual and ritual beliefs. The men with the most power are the shamans who are chosen by the principal power spirit Kain Dyen Ngop. The next most powerful are the ritual specialists, and then healers and sorcerers. These are followed by the initiated males having no spirit-associated special function but who are full members of the male pandanas cult. Finally, there are the noninitiates, women, and children of either sex below nine or ten years old.

---

[6]Infanticide results from different motivations not all related to a struggle for power or influence within a marriage. However, even in very recent times, infanticide has been practiced as a means of punishing or hurting men. It appears that the greatest number of infanticides (for whatever motive) are of female children.

The Spirits

The diagram in figure 5 lists the categories of spirits recognized by the Ketengban and their relative importance, authority, power, and origin. In the diagram, higher vertical ranking indicates greater authority and length of existence. Spirits on the same level are equal in power and came into existence at about the same time. A solid line joining two categories indicates that the second is derived from the first. The spirit categories are discussed as discrete entities, but the Ketengban do not systematize information in this way. The timing and relationships between the various eras and beings are not always clear, even to the Ketengban who related it to us. The spirit categories are described starting from the top of the chart.

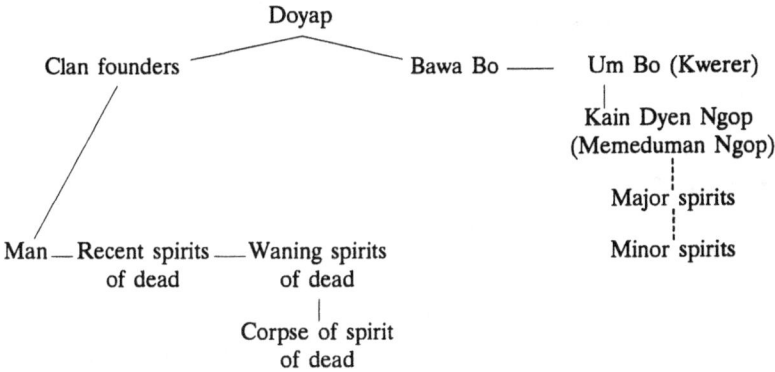

Fig. 5. Ketengban spirit categories

31

The Creator (*doyap*)

The earliest known being who resided on top of Mount Mandala (*limgonai*) is called *doyap* (or *duyap*). He created the physical universe, including humans and animals. Due to this foundational accomplishment, he is also known by several secret names including *limdoyap* 'Doyap of Lim Mountain', *nimi deiyo ngop* 'man who is the source of men', *nimi nai ngop* 'father of man', and *nimi kweimdim ngop* 'creator of man'. Like many creator deities in Melanesian mythology (Habel 1979), Doyap created the universe, then disappeared, and is no longer active in the daily life of his creation. He delegated the responsibility for maintaining life and order to other spirits. Though it is said that Doyap created all that is, the detailed description of his activities refers to the western quarter of Ketengban territory. This, too, is typical of Melanesian mythological figures who create one key geographical area. However, Doyap's creation includes the traditional areas of all the Ketengban clans and all their clan founders. Doyap's location during creation, place of retirement, and current residence is Limgonai, and its center is the ice cap of Mount Mandala.

First, Doyap made two very large bodies of water, *bime* and *tanime*, which began to pool and then became quite large. During this process Doyap created everything visible including people, flora, and fauna, everything found in the sky or on land. During this period Doyap's sister and brothers were living with him, but had nothing to do with creation. His brothers were *limtola* and *kwerer* (also known as *lim kwerer*) and his sister was *limkwerepkor ner*.

While Limtola and Doyap were on top of Limgonai mountain having a conversation, the Bime and Tanime waters began to argue about which would be first to overflow the holding area into the valleys Doyap created. All created things were now floating on the waters and as Doyap and Limtola talked, finally the Bime water broke free first, being greater in mass and more powerful, and rushed down the mountainside in a great wall of water. This great flood carried the most prized items of Doyap's creation including people, pandanas, prized banana species, sago, and animals. This water flowed into the Bidoman area, i.e., the Bime river valley system. The Tanime waters overflowed next but went toward the western and northern lowlands taking the residue of created things, such as sago, cassowaries, fish, and a few people. Details of subsequent events in that area are not known to the highland Ketengban.

Doyap and his brothers followed the great rush of water and resulting landslide down from the mountaintop to the Bime river valley system, deciding to finish the dispersion and assigning of things from there. Kwerer was primarily responsible for this. He saw that if he did not quickly intervene all the best things would flow out the northwesternmost lowland valley openings and be too widely scattered. His intention was to have the best things and majority of the population within the Bime valley system, so he quickly placed his hardwood brush-cutting "blade" in the narrow neck of the lowest valley mouth damming up the Bime waters and stopping the flow of things it carried. This stage constituted the first major division of creation.

Kwerer also had the responsibility of assigning lands, social responsibilities, and ritual authority, thus ordering life for all creation. He assigned totem animals, birds, or reptiles embodying a companion spirit to each established clan. Doyap, as the oldest and most powerful deity, began to prepare the first spirit house with the help of Limtola and Kwerepkor Ner at a place called Bopgon, Mergekin, or Monggonirye. It became the most important spirit house (*bopgon ati* or *mergekin ati*) and is the site where the initiation cycle always begins (see figure 6).

As his initial act in building the spirit house, Doyap planted the first ironwood house pole, which was found in the debris carried down in the flood from Limgonai. He gave instructions for finishing the house and then went to place the support poles for two additional spirit houses in two nearby areas, *depesaban* and *peremgonban*.

After Doyap had gone (not to return again), his sister Kwerepkor Ner began to have children. These children were all man-eating female spirits which became the most malevolent and powerful spirits of the land. One of them was an extremely important spirit, *ketlingna ner,* who was instrumental in multiplying the inhabitants of the land.

Also present during this primordial era were a few of the clan founders or progenitors: a Wisal woman, a Lepitalen man, a Monggon man, a Kipka woman, a Meikku man, and a few others. While Kwerepkor Ner was bearing female children, her brother Kwerer, along with the Wisal woman and Lepitalen and Meiku men, went back to the original spirit house site, Bopgon. These three first clan founders had decided to follow Kwerer's instructions to hold an initiation for young men. They put all the initiates up in a tree on some fern leaves and were dancing and holding the initiation ceremony underneath the tree. After a very long time, the initiates became dehydrated (having no water to drink), filthy, emaciated, and covered with flies. Excrement had also accumulated under their tree. Trying to better their situation, the Lepitalen man killed a marsupial (cuscus) and gave it to them to eat. But since there was no fire yet, they

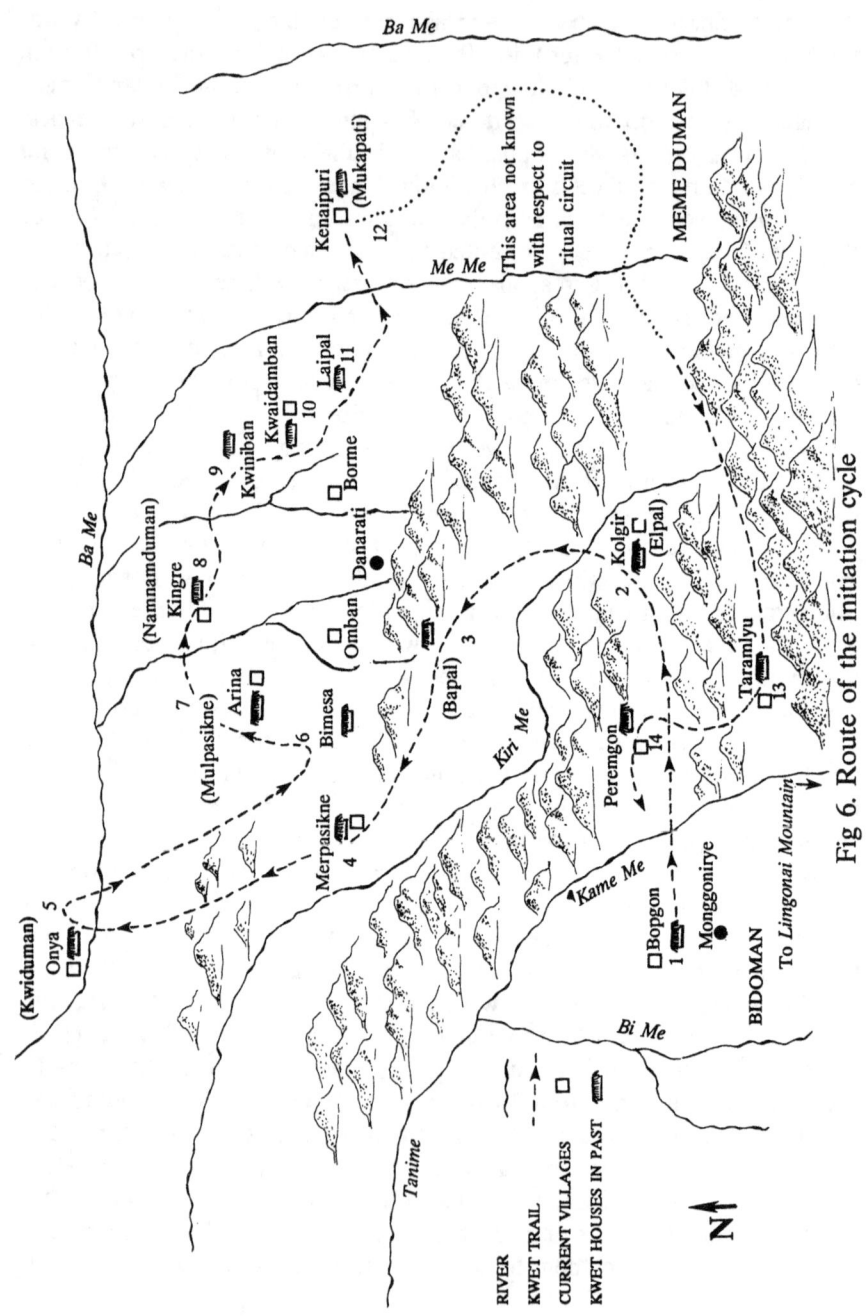

Fig 6. Route of the initiation cycle

had to eat it raw, and it only worsened their condition. At this point, Kwerer came and saw the terrible situation. This led to the next stage of development and the most critical event in preserving the life and ceremonial-social order of the Ketengban people.

Sacrificial Deity (*um bo*)

Doyap's brother, Kwerer, is of a type found in many Melanesian cultures, classified by some as a Dema deity (Flannery 1979), whose death turned into a creative process and whose essence remains in the items involved in his death. Further, the Ketengban partake of his essence during the ritual pig feasts he established as part of their life.

At this point in the mythology, a major transformation took place. When Kwerer came and saw the terrible situation resulting from the people's attempts to hold the first initiation according to his instructions, he proclaimed two things: first, that his name be changed from Kwerer to Um Bo, (in some accounts *umpe*), and second, that a radical intervention was the only way to repair the damage and allow life to go on. Um Bo (Kwerer) told the Wisal woman and the others that putting the initiates up in the tree was wrong and this practice had caused the boys' skins to dry up and leave them in a despicable condition. Then he announced that he would give his own life and body as a sacrifice to repair the damage. Then Kwerer, who was now Um Bo, instructed the Wisal woman to kill him, cut up his body, and render the grease from his inner parts. The people were to take the grease and rub it over the dried ruined skins of the initiates to restore them. Furthermore, a ritual representing this act was to be repeated for men everywhere in perpetuity, and Um Bo gave specific instructions for the process and attendant ceremonies.

Then the Wisal woman took a pig rope (*bisam turya*); tied Um Bo to a *dekne* tree, and shot him with a bow and arrow. When the arrow hit Um Bo, he became an enormous pig and, screaming shrilly from the fatal wound, leapt into the air breaking the pig rope. Now bleeding in his death throes, Um Bo bounded through the air in a great circular path throughout Ketengban territory, stopping briefly in numerous places. Each place where he landed became a clan center, a key initiation house, or another important ritual house. Among others he landed at Yapinimban, Paumban, Keraperban, Malkondam, Souplelyu, Depesaban, and finally returned to Bopgon or Monggonirye where Doyap had begun the first spirit house. In many of these places he did something characteristic of dying pigs, such as squealing, urinating, bleeding, defecating, and rolling in a pool with each such action usually reflected in the name of these important places.

Finally the people at the initiation/killing site heard a great commotion coming from the Depesaban area and said to the Lepitalen man, "Since you are of the dog totem and can thus run faster than we can without tiring, you go there to see if he has died at Depesaban." So the Lepitalen man ran up there and saw Um Bo was dying, but when the Lepitalen man said he would go and report it, Um Bo told him not to do so. He wanted to return to the original spirit house site at Monggonirye and die there.

Upon arriving at Monggonirye, Um Bo instructed the Lepitalen man to divide up his body (now in the form of a large pig) and then he died. In accordance with his instructions, the Lepitalen man cut off the leg (which had been the arm) on which Um Bo, when he was still Kwerer, had tied his fire-starting vine (*sekne*). He then stood aside as the Wisal woman finished cutting up Um Bo's pig body. After steaming his parts in the cooking pit, the Wisal woman and Monggon man took them out and finished dividing the portions and laying them in display for distribution among those present. This type of display at feasts remained important throughout their ritual-dominated past and can even be seen to a degree today.

The names of many other clans began at this feast since their names are words which recall the part their founders played in this process. For example, one woman collected small bits of discarded meat, bone, and fat and put them in a net bag while the larger portions were being displayed. The verb *kina* 'putting into a net bag' has as its far past singular form *kipke*, and the clan name used for the descendants of that woman is *kipka*. Another person present handed razor-sharp pieces of bamboo, traditionally used as knives, to those cutting up Um Bo's pig body. The Ketengban word for bamboo knife is *pa*, an older secret word for cutting instruments is *yoma*, and these words combine into the clan name for this person's descendants, *payumka*. There are many names formed on this kind of pattern.

Before all the displayed pieces could be handed out, Um Bo sent a sudden strong wind. The wind blew the pieces of meat, fat, and the people watching or holding them into the air, and they all came down in the places where Kwerer had previously decided they should be. Many of these places where pieces of Um Bo's pig body landed, with or without people holding them, became population centers or important locations for ceremonial-ritual houses. The names of these locations often refer to that particular body portion. For instance, *taram yo* means 'breast bone' and the place where that portion of Um Bo fell is called *taramlyu*. The word for 'neck' is *kume* and the village area where it landed is called *kumkarye*. All the progenitors were thus dispersed to what is now their traditional land, many of them places where Um Bo had fallen during his death throes. They took with them portions of Um Bo's body containing his power and essence, and placed them in the spirit houses they built. They were to symbolically partake of Um Bo's essence in every pig feast, ceremonial or common, throughout all later generations.

Another major transformation took place upon the death of Um Bo. When Um Bo allowed himself to be killed to restore good skins to the initiates and ensure continuing life for the people, he released his spirit or became a spirit. Only his body as Kwerer-Um Bo died, because his essence is eternal. Upon death he was transformed to an immensely powerful spirit known as *kain dyen ngop* 'the pandanas eating man' which rules all other spirits.

Two other events resulted from deep grief over Um Bo's death. His brother, Limtola, became so saddened that he left the area and went down to the lowland area where the great Tanime water flowed. The highland people know little else about him though people from the Tanime river system could probably relate his story. The culture hero, Bawa Bo, was so deeply grieved that he went under the earth's surface and entered a deep sleep.

Ruler Spirit (*kain dyen ngop*)

The spirit of Um Bo, Kain Dyen Ngop, is the most powerful spirit and he rules all other spirits.[7] Though most propitiation and petitioning of

---

[7]There are slightly differing versions of Ketengban mythology from different dialect or geographical areas. This is not surprising since regular outside contacts began for these people only in 1972. Previous to that time warfare, aspects of the social system, their spirit beliefs, and the rugged terrain limited travel and sharing of information between areas. Some mythological accounts mention a ruler spirit called Memeduman Ngop. His name usually occurs in connection with the eastern third of Ketengban territory. I suspect that he is the eastern equivalent of the central and western Kain Dyen Ngop, and perhaps he was incorporated into these accounts as men heard his name mentioned as a powerful spirit. Details of his origins are not available in the area of our research, but the deeds attributed to him in relation to men parallel those of Kain Dyen Ngop. Therefore, Kain Dyen Ngop and Memeduman Ngop are either the same spirit known by different names or two different spirits of equivalent power, but the lack of additional information about Memeduman Ngop prevents a conclusion at this time.

spirits is done with reference to Um Bo, his closest connection now with humans is his spirit Kain Dyen Ngop and all must be done through him, though in Um Bo's honor.

There is a key difference between Um Bo's character before his sacrificial death and what he is now as Kain Dyen Ngop (see figure 7). Um Bo was benevolently concerned with the welfare of man. He established Ketengban social order and ritual life. In the end he gave his life and substance to restore the first initiates and complete the ceremony without which boys could not become men, and life could not be lived in harmony with the universe. Kain Dyen Ngop, on the other hand, is characterized by a mean and angry disposition. He strikes fear into Ketengban hearts by being prone to cause disaster and death for even minor infractions or slights to his honor. There is a never-ending necessity to placate him. He is described as evil and capricious whereas Um Bo is never referred to in this way. This dichotomy parallels the way humans and the spirits of the dead are characterized: the living person may have been a jovial, generous person, but his spirit is likely to be dangerous. The visible and tangible is usually predictable and good, but the unseen tends to be malevolent.

	Kwerer	Um Bo	Kain Dyen Ngop
Form	man-like	pig	spirit
Responsibility	ordered life	sacrificed himself	head of evil spirits
Nature	disinterested	benefactor	evil, avenging
Human Response	passive	honoring, obeying	placating, appeasing

Fig. 7. Progression in identity of Kwerer (Doyap's brother)

Kain Dyen Ngop is like men in some respects. He decorates himself with feathers, ear plugs, and other ornamentation. A certain type of pandanas, an important ceremonial food with which he is particularly concerned, is his dancing ornament. This variety of pandanas (*alem kain*) is very long, straight, and red, and men want their dancing ornaments and pandanas to meet these same standards (see figure 8).

This dancing ornamentation is worn around the neck hanging down the back. Kain Dyen Ngop also wears colorful net bags decorated with feathers, uses nose bones, necklaces, arm and leg bands, and carries a bow and arrows with which to shoot men. He can give these arrows to other spirits to use. He has gardens, and though he has no wives, he does have many younger sisters. His children are those humans whom he has chosen for spirit mediation (*asuru kwa neng*) or to be ritual specialists (*mem deiyo neng*).

Though greatly feared, he is respected as the sustainer of life. He never forgets, and if made angry will certainly punish, either directly or through the spirits under him. Though not omnipresent, he can move quickly and travels constantly. His habitations include certain huge rocks or large trees like the *gu, bor, wa,* and *irik*. His essence remains in the pandanas mentioned earlier and is able to take this form, in which manifestation he is secretly called *emdam ngop* 'near the pandanus one'.

He or his essence also inhabits the major ceremonial and initiation houses (*mem ati*) and taboo places (*mem mutu*) such as Bopgon, Dopolban, Dangar, Namnamban, Depesaban, and Elpal.

Kain Dyen Ngop is jealously concerned with the proper running of the social order and ritual-ceremonial life which, as Um Bo, he gave instructions for and set in motion. He is the spirit from whom all other spirits must get permission to do their good or evil. He ultimately polices and judges all of life and controls all prosperity and production.

The companion spirits of the clans and male heads of spirit houses are assigned by him and are under his rule and jurisdiction. The sorcerers, spirit mediators, diviners, and other ritual specialists receive their instructions from him. The clan companion spirits report oversights and misdeeds to him and he gives permission to punish or kill, or does so himself.

Fig. 8. Dancing ornamentation related to Kain Dyen Ngop

Because of the close relationship between Kain Dyen Ngop and the ceremonial-ritual life of the Ketengban people, further details about him may be found in the section on Rituals.

Major Spirits

The three distinguishing characteristics of major spirits are that they are female, originate from the earliest era, and are fiercely malevolent. These spirits are the daughters of Doyap's sister. Relative to man or ancestral spirits, they are preexistent and eternal. They were never human beings nor do they inhabit or possess humans or give power to them. Further, they are extremely powerful and dangerous to male human beings and are described as man-eating. Though they may be enticed to help people by certain rituals or food gifts, they are almost exclusively responsible for sickness, death, and calamities to both men and women.

As previously explained, the two principal power spirits are Kain Dyen Ngop and Memeduman Ngop. Though Kain Dyen Ngop is the supreme ruler of all spirits, Memeduman Ngop has nearly equivalent powers over the major spirits assigned to him, and it is possible that he is simply the eastern dialect equivalent of Kain Dyen Ngop. Both of these highest ranking principal spirits (*nimi kamaya*) have a large group of powerful female spirits under their direction. Both the *kamaya* and the *isok ner* 'female spirits' come up into the realm of man through the holes in hollow trees or near special sites. They then travel through the sky or return to the tunnels under the earth's surface to reach their next destination. These female spirits are always moving, watching, and listening for infractions of Um Bo's regulations and looking for people's hearts and spirits to eat. Though killing is their main business, it is usually because of some wrongdoing on the victim's part. Eating a person's spirit does not cause a special relationship between one of the female spirits and the victim, nor is the spirit completely removed from the body. The female spirit eats the essence of her victim, so the person dies.

Though the permission of Kain Dyen Ngop and Memeduman Ngop must be gained to cause sickness and death, the work itself is done by one of these malevolent female spirits unless the two principal power spirits are extremely angry with the person and wish to kill them personally. If sudden catastrophic illness or death strikes, it is a sign that Kain Dyen Ngop or Memeduman Ngop is directly responsible. If sickness and prolonged suffering end in a slower death, then it is caused by one of the malevolent female spirits. Experienced diviners may recognize individual sicknesses as the work of certain ones of these female spirits.

It is necessary to determine which spirits are causing trouble or carrying out punishments at a given time. Since rituals, including those used for healing, have been assigned to various clans, once the origin of a sickness has been determined, it is usually necessary to find a person from the clan with the particular incantation or skill necessary to perform the ritual on the basis of their relationship to their totem spirits. A person's own clansmen may be powerless if the calamity is caused by spirits associated with a different clan or if the necessary incantations are owned and carried out only by a different clan. However, spirit dominance is not rigidly delineated and the spirits may cooperate across group or clan lines.

If a spirit related to a particular clan cannot carry out a requested killing or some other curse alone, she may cooperate with other powerful area spirits to do it. Spirits do not fight among themselves as humans do, but may have arguments at times about killing people, although some arrangement is usually reached and the killing accomplished. Each major spirit has a specific name or names, most of which are known only to spirit headmen, spirit mediators, sorcerers, and healers. The names usually give a main characteristic of the spirit or information about her habitat or actions. There are too many of these spirits to describe individually, but a few will serve as representative examples.

(1) *limusukor ner* 'coming-down-from-Limgonai-mountain woman' has several other names depending on her actions or point of departure and is very dangerous. As Limusukor Ner, she is always seeking people who are weak or becoming ill from the action of other spirits. When such a person is found, she sits outside their house and sniffs the air like a dog or a pig. Sick people have an odor detectable to spirits just as ripe fruit attracts bats. Such people are called "ripe," using the same word as is applied to fruit. Limusukor Ner sniffs to find the person and then enters the house to eat the essence of the victim's heart (*talema, dipru*) or spirit (*sambala*) causing their death. If, however, a shaman is available who is able to see her sitting near the house, he will usually advise that the sick person be taken out and left in the jungle. There Limusukor Ner can eat the spirit without having the chance to see others she might also want to eat. This spirit is also known as *ketlingna ner* 'travels-all-about-like-the-sun woman' as a reminder that she travels to many areas and participates in the feasting and dancing at the major initiation ceremonies.

Ketlingna Ner has an insatiable appetite for pig and other small animals. Being quickly dissatisfied with offerings at ceremonial times, she is likely to cause sickness, especially a disease where the victim gradually declines until death. She particularly watches that no one kills and eats pigs without honoring Kain Dyen Ngop and offering some to him. If they do not, such offenders or their relatives become sick. If proper offerings are made but the site improperly cleared of evidence of this secret ritual, then she again causes sickness and death. This evidence could be bits of banana leaves with pig grease on them, burnt wood, or arrowheads laying about where they could be observed by noninitiates instead of being carefully hidden or destroyed in the fire. Such careless, disrespectful acts incite her to rise from the ground nearby and inflict sickness.

(2) *nimi dipru doropkor ner* 'she-is-going-to-take-men's-hearts-out woman' or *bondam ner* 'near-holes woman' is likely to come out of small holes in man's realm to eat people's spirits. Such holes are usually near trees or fire poles of a men's house and, though normally invisible to common men, any small dark hole is suspect.

(3) *ungka ner* is another female spirit who brings sickness and eats the breath, speech, heart, or blood of a person, resulting in death.

(4) *manarkor ner* is the spirit responsible for the growth and fertility of pigs. Whenever pigs are to be killed, she has to be informed in advance, in order to avoid the appearance of a person exhibiting too much self-initiative which would be dishonoring to her. Slighting her this way implies the intention of feasting on the pig wihout giving some to Kain Dyen Ngop or Memeduman Ngop and the spirits of relatives. Although pigs are the most valuable items of exchange, especially for bride price, sometimes it is necessary to set aside other items for her. The person places pig meat and other bride exchange items in her honor on the special shelf on the wall across from the door of the men's house. Failure to do so angers her, bringing retaliation in the form of sickness in pigs or people or a refusal to help women raise their pigs, resulting in sickness, mange, runny eyes, and death for these pigs. This failure causes financial insecurity and has serious long range consequences, such as the inability to offer appropriate spirit sacrifices, make good bride payments, and enter into mutually benefi- cial obligations and alliances with others.

(5) Two other major female spirits are *olelum nunupkor ner* 'from-Ole- waterfall woman' and *olelum kunka ner* 'she-is-going-to-be-at-Ole-waterfall woman'. Though spirits which frequent certain locations are discussed elsewhere, these two are distinct due to their greater power and activity.

Olelum Nunupkor Ner approaches villages and looks in at the men seated in the men's house. She can cause diarrhea, other intestinal ailments, or huge swellings of their faces and noses. Her partner, Olelum Kunka Ner, comes after other spirits have caused sickness and death and cuts up the body when it has been placed in the tree. She divides the body with other spirits who come but when they leave she takes out the intestines, cleans them, and eats them raw. She employs a similar tactic with living people who are sickly, taking their intestines, straightening them out, and squeezing the contents into her mouth. After that, the victims announce that their breath is leaving and they are soon to die. The victims experience great pain and become hysterical, jumping up, moaning and yelling, and pounding the house walls in their death throes. This activity is a sign that Olelum Kunka Ner (secret name) or *olelumdam ner* 'the woman near Ole waterfall' (common name) caused the illness.

These two spirits also frequent burial areas of the Dipur, Wisal, and Monggon clans. From there they seek "ripe" sickly people, so those burial places are avoided. If these spirits should enter the abdomen of a person visiting burial areas, that person becomes a "carrier" and the spirits return with them to the village, causing all the people there to die.

Though there are many such spirits, the evil work they perform is much the same, causing sickness or calamity, and eventually eating or stealing the spirits, hearts, or other vital parts of people, causing their death. These spirits respond quickly and viciously to infractions of respect, honor, or sacrifice protocol, and obey the principal spirits' wishes to punish people. They sometimes capriciously kill people on their own, although usually the victim has done something wrong. But they never do anything for people on their own initiative. Such requests by human beings, usually to cause someone else's death, have to be sought with long-term giving of pig or other foods and by the correct recitation of certain incantations. Although it is possible to entreat these spirits, it is not possible to force their compliance even with the correct prescribed rituals. If they are pleased and happy with the offerings, they might be disposed to grant the supplicant's wishes unless certain shamans and healers who have direct contact with the principal power spirits stop or reverse their actions. These spirits sometimes use the services of shamans, providing them with spirit arrows to shoot into people and then leaving the final decision of whether or not to kill them in the shamans' hands.

The major Ketengban spirits do not play mischievous pranks but are deadly serious. They will, however, give hints of impending doom to people, frightening them. For instance, they might invisibly touch someone with their cold hands, signalling that death is near. Or if a corpse is in the house with relatives before being put up in the tree, its eyes might suddenly open and look at a specific person, indicating the approaching death of that person. This action signifies that the dead person's spirit has met the female spirit and heard this information directly. If a shaman sees a spirit sitting outside a house and looks inside at the people sitting there, the one about to die appears as though his skin has been burned off and only bones remain.

As another sign of coming death, the spirits can leave charcoal in a person's net bag or place a bit of it in the eating container in front of the victim. As the people squat around the food eating, the victim, eventually finding the charcoal in his portion, is warned of impending death. If signalled by charcoal, death is a certainty and nothing can be done to stop it, even though the principal power spirits allowed the major spirits to warn the victim. The spirits sometimes slyly cause people to make a deadly mistake by leaving a pandanas leaf, stick, or piece of bamboo on a trail or place where the intended victim will pass. When the unsuspecting person removes it or brushes it aside, he triggers his own death. These spirits can also kill people by natural disasters such as flash floods, landslides, and falling trees or rocks.

When people wish to do evil to others, they either ask the spirits with whom they have a good relationship or an intermediary to get a sorcerer to entreat the spirits, paying him later with a stone axe, piglet, or other valuable. The middleman later gives either part or all of it to the sorcerer. Contracting for a death is called *bul dokotena* 'sending coldness', and the indirect method is often used if the particular spirit needed is related to another clan.

One major male spirit who has a special place and function is *limdepunge* 'the one who died at Lim mountain long ago'. He is also called *limtungmop* 'the rotten, stinking man of Lim', *limbulungyap* 'the cold man of Lim', *limkwirimop* 'the staring-eye man of Lim', or *dena deiyo ngop* 'the source-of-death man'. Only the last name listed is not taboo and can be spoken in front of the uninitiated.

When Doyap created all things, but before the flood of waters swept everything off Limgonai mountain, he also made Limdepunge, then a man. Limdepunge was ordained to be the first man to die and then to become the headman of death. All the spirits of the dead are under him and considered to be his children, along with a few special death-related spirits who live near the mountaintops. If he had not died or had been able to change his skin, then mankind also would not die, but because Doyap created him, all people die. Unlike Melanesian myths attributing death to a stupid mistake (Flannery 1979), the Ketengban say that man was destined for death by Doyap.

Death occurs when a major spirit (not Limdepunge), or Kain Dyen Ngop, or Memeduman Ngop causes sickness and eats someone's spirit, heart, or other vital part. When this process is completed, the spirit which brings death itself is Limdepunge or his subordinates, such as *dening, denbulung isok, potongyawa,* or *parumbuna*.

In summary, there are many major Ketengban spirits, most of which are the daughters of Doyap's sister and are extremely powerful, malevolent, and greatly feared. They function as subordinates to Kain Dyen Ngop or Memeduman Ngop and carry out their bidding, policing men's affairs and punishing transgressions and insults to themselves or their superiors by eating people's vital parts, causing sickness and weakness. Eventually, death itself is accomplished by Limdepunge and his helpers.

Minor Spirits

Spirits categorized as minor spirits in this paper are similar to those called nature spirits in other areas of Melanesia (Habel 1979). They are not powerful like the major spirits just discussed nor are they deities. Though some were present in the primordial era, none have clear origins like the female children of Kwerepkor Ner. They are described in terms of their usual locality or actions. These minor spirits, although clearly evil and capable of causing serious problems and even death, are more likely to cause less deadly mischief. Their power and activities vary, but none are as fearsome as those designated herein as major spirits. None of them take human form to trick or seduce people except for one minor spirit which does seduce young unmarried women. Though they are often linked to certain characteristic places or things, and some have animal forms, none have been described as the spirit of the waters, spirit of the trees, or spirit of a particular animal. They simply frequent those places or have the forms of the animals.

There appear to be two subsets of these minor spirits although these distinctions are not articulated as such by the Ketengban. The spirits in animal form tend to be more powerful, while the less powerful spirits are usually encountered in certain places or things. None of these spirits initiate action but rather are messengers of the companion spirits, the principal power spirits, and the major female spirits, reporting to them and doing their bidding.

Of those spirits in animal, reptile, or bird form, the two most feared and powerful are *tau pena*, who appears as a certain taboo cuscus (marsupial), (also known secretly as *bumgetekna, waiya, aiyamop,* or *aiya*) and *nimi dyen bisam* 'man-eating pig', who appears in the form of a large voracious pig. Three others worthy of mention are in the forms of the *weri* bird, the *ibi* or *sanip* cassowary, and the small *alseksekmope* cuscus.

Tau Pena is the most commonly encountered minor spirit because he is the policeman and helper of every men's house, residing in a special place high on the wall directly across from the doorway. This position enables him to see everything, including what takes place just outside the house, and also puts him in an honored position above everyone, making it impossible for anyone to pass behind him or to enter without being reminded of him. His job is to carefully watch the members and activities of the men's house, especially in regard to food consumption. His concern is that the proper gifts be given and rituals performed in honor of Kain Dyen Ngop and also that food be shared with the ancestors. Food, especially ceremonially important foods like pandanas and pork, can never be eaten casually. There is always a ritual to be performed, an incantation to be said, or some portion to be given to Tau Pena and thus by extension to Kain Dyen Ngop or Memeduman Ngop. In addition, the ancestral spirits have to be honored by food portions. Larger food items like big taro, pandanas, or pork are never to be eaten outside the hamlet or men's house unless for a specially designated ritual or ceremony. Small portions of less-prized foods can be eaten in gardens or jungle houses, but a portion has to be brought back to share in the men's house. Therefore, Tau Pena is always looking for food coming into the house or evidence that food has been eaten outside and not legitimized by proper ritual. Gift portions of food, pork, or tobacco are often placed on his wall perch and he either "eats" the essence of this himself or safeguards it for Kain Dyen Ngop or Memeduman Ngop's return.

He is limited to being at home and cannot travel, but this limitation is offset because the spirits of the dead are very mobile and report infractions to him. The spirit of a man's dead father could report to Tau Pena that his son ate food in the jungle and did not bring a portion for the ancestors, asking Tau Pena to have him made ill or killed. Tau Pena would become angry over the arrogance of ignoring the two principal power spirits (and the snub to himself) and would pout, cry, and turn his back on those in the house. When Kain Dyen Ngop or Memeduman Ngop returns from his travels, this illicit disrespectful food consumption would be reported to him by Tau Pena. Kain Dyen Ngop or Memeduman Ngop could then punish the offenders as previously described or could decide to use Tau Pena, who would then "grip the person with his teeth and claws." Tau Pena also has some responsibility for large taro and potato gardens, helping to make them more fruitful.

The second most powerful minor spirit is *nimi dyen bisam* 'man eating pig'. His secret names are *engdopu, mokupapu, uritungtung,* and *mukup doptutupu bisam,* which reflect his characteristics and his actions. They mean 'taking the ripe (ones)', 'cramming into his mouth', 'very black one from Uri mountain', and 'he came from Mukup spirit house following and interfering with men'. This pig spirit is owned and cared for by Kain Dyen Ngop or Memeduman Ngop and has a red streak painted on his cheek to mark this ownership.

When corpses are finally placed high in a tree, this spirit pig comes from a hole near the tree or a hole near a special pole planted there. Having smelled the "ripeness" of the corpse, he eats the spirit and/or body of the person or roots around the tree or pole causing the body to fall down to the ground, which is extremely disrespectful. Another problem posed by this pig spirit is related to the outcroppings of rock near the doorways of certain ceremonial or ritual houses. Since these outcroppings go deep underground and cannot be moved, it is believed that they are the snout of this pig, although it is never mentioned lest it anger him.[8] If certain rituals are not carried out correctly, then he will open his enormous mouth, and all those present (and perhaps people everywhere) will fall in and be consumed. During another ritual ensuring plentiful harvests, water spurts from a spring carrying items used for garden fertility. This water is believed to be coming from this pig spirit's nostrils and penis because of its constricted nature, quantity, and forcefulness.

This same pig spirit also helps in obtaining rattan vine needed for part of another ceremony. This particular species of vine (*tawar tapke*) is essential because Um Bo had wrapped it around his arm as a fire-starting vine. When hunting this vine, it is auspicious to find some with the roots

---

[8]At certain times these rock outcroppings are rubbed with pig grease, and special rites are chanted to calm the great pig in much the same way that one can rub the snout or stomach of a domestic pig to pleasure him and calm him down.

already severed near the ground or with the topmost leaves already withered. This is evidence that the pig spirit had cut it, and things will go well in the ceremony. Repeating the pig spirit's name so that he will be pleased and not open his mouth, the people then happily bring the vine to the ceremonial house.

A less powerful spirit in cassowary form is *sanipe,* or *ibi.* This cassowary spirit, like the pig spirit, is larger than normal. Sometime in the far past Um Bo realized how powerful the cassowary was and sent him down to the lowlands where fewer people live and the ground is flatter and less rocky. When the cassowary is angry, it aggressively kicks with its powerful legs, and the highlanders believe this action could cause large rocks to dislodge and fall, killing people and destroying gardens.

The sanipe cassowary spirit is a messenger from Kain Dyen Ngop or Memeduman Ngop of impending doom, making a sound reminiscent of a distinctive cassowary noise. Again, when angered, a cassowary will make a sudden forceful sound in its throat while jerking its vestigial wings up. (The sound is alarming, somewhat reminiscent of pulling apart a large piece of velcro simultaneously with rushing air and a "pop.") When a person has done wrong, Kain Dyen Ngop will sometimes send a warning by calling the cassowary spirit in the lowlands to bring his large bow. A sudden ear-splitting clap of thunder directly over someone's roof is actually this cassowary spirit snapping his bowstring. It resembles the sound a normal cassowary makes. The Ketengban liken it to being slapped hard on the ears or on the head by a huge hand. This is Kain Dyen Ngop's punishment to the offender and his relatives in the house with him, but is also a harbinger of sickness and death.

Such a warning is merited if someone in the house (or a relative) has killed a person who honored Kain Dyen Ngop or Memeduman Ngop and who was his *mawa* 'to keep possession' or *mi sisa* 'real child'.

Another cause for rebuke is surreptitiously eating food items either of remarkable size or growing in plain view in gardens or near houses without honoring the spirits and sharing the food. If these items are from the jungle and of unremarkable size (excepting pandanas, pork, and taro), they might be eaten secretly without angering Kain Dyen Ngop. However, because many people have seen this food and perhaps commented on its special size or quality and will recognize that it is missing, this behavior is selfish and disrespectful. The power of the cassowary spirit is also recalled in several items used in some of the rituals.

Four other less powerful and less active spirits are the sago palm cuscus, the snake, the *weri* bird 'rainbow lorikeet', and the lowland river creatures such as eel-fish, fresh water crabs, and prawns.

The cuscus (*alseksekmope*) characteristically lives among sago palm fronds and thickets. There are extensive sago swamps in lowland Ketengban territory, and many sago palms have been planted in wet areas as high as 4,000 feet above sea level. This spirit does not travel much, but must be remembered and appeased whenever normal houses and shelters or ceremonial and ritual houses are built. Since sago palms are frequently used as thatching material, this spirit is encountered while collecting thatch. When thatch is carried to the building site of any spirit house, the cuscus spirit rides in the thatch. When the thatch is incorporated into the roof, it is said to represent the spirit's hair or fur. Only men from the Basiduman clan grouping can collect these fronds for certain ceremonial houses because of their specially assigned association with this spirit. The cuscus spirit can be placated and pleased by being given raw meat while incantations are recited, which have variations on "I am taking your hair" and repeating his name.

The minor spirit chosen to represent those in the form of birds is the rainbow lorikeet (*weri*). This bird spirit watches for those who transgress Um Bo's pandanas-eating protocol at important feasts, rituals, and ceremonies. The Lepitalen clan has the privilege and responsibility of eating pandanas before anyone else. Similarly, when pandanas ripens, the Lepitalen clan has the right to pick the first ones for the whole territory, and only then are other clans permitted to pick pandanas. Should anyone disobey these two regulations, the *weri* spirit punishes them and reports it to Kain Dyen Ngop or Memeduman Ngop. The *weri* will choke the offender with its talons and sharp beak causing discomfort, difficulty in eating, and even death.

In the lower elevations where the rushing, tumbling streams slow down to form pools, there are minor spirits which may take the form of a certain fish, eel, fresh water prawn, or crab. The fish here is common to many Irian Jaya rivers and has whiskers resembling a catfish but is black, has more slimy skin, and has a dorsal fin on its back and a fin on its stomach extending its entire length. This makes it look like an eel with the head of a catfish. All these water creatures embody the same minor spirit, which cooperates with the spirits of the dead or with major spirits in finding certain "ripe" people whose spirits can be eaten, such as newborns, new mothers, menstruating women, or their relatives. They sense tiny bits of food, body dirt, blood, or vernix (washed off newborns) in the waters that flow by them. These bits of matter associated with humans attract these spirits who either report it and its human source to the major spirits and the spirits of the dead or follow the scent trail and come themselves to cause sickness and possible death.

The second subset of minor spirits differ from the first, not in their activities, but in that they are characteristically found in certain areas and take no special shape.

The first of these is the *kambop neng* spirits who are encountered near mountain peaks and ridgetops and are known to live particularly in thickets of a broadleafed plant (*omgala*) which grows in poor soil near ridgetops or rock outcroppings.[9] The *kambop neng* spirits can also be found in ferns growing on cliff faces or near waterfalls and sometimes come to villages to cause trouble.

This set of spirits can cause madness and irrational behavior in people. Sometimes the shamans make use of this power and take the invisible "children" of these spirits off the wall in a men's house and throw them into a group of men, causing everyone to become temporarily possessed and to speak in ecstatic languages. The *kambop neng* cause trouble when they come down into hamlets during the night and have sexual relations with attractive unmarried girls, resulting in various social problems and tensions when the girls either become pregnant or demonstrate behavioral changes commensurate with illicit sexual relationships.

Another type of frequently encountered minor spirit lives near waterfalls, especially the many large spectacular ones common in the Ketengban area. Each spirit's name basically means 'the spirit woman near such-and-such waterfall'. For example, the mountain with the largest waterfall is *ate,* the word for waterfall is *me lum,* and the words for 'near' and 'woman' are *dam* and *ner,* respectively. This Ate spirit's name is thus *ate melumdam ner* 'the spirit woman living near the Ate mountain waterfall'. Some better known spirits of this type are *ure melumdam ner, ole melumdam ner* or *olelum kunka ner, pale lumdam ner,* and *wayo lumdam ner* where the first word is the mountain's name. These waterfalls are usually in remote places, and travel near them is uncommon. These spirits cause people to fall off the cliff faces near their waterfalls or they bring a polio-like withering of the legs in men and vaginal bleeding in women, all of which can result in death.

---

[9]The *omgala* plant recalls the primordial era in that this was the leaf on which the first initiates were seated up in the tree when Um Bo decided to sacrifice himself.

A more subtle and likely danger results from coveting property guarded by these spirits. If someone traveling through the jungle sees a desirable thing, such as eggs from a jungle chicken or crown pigeon (*lyei ma*), or a tree whose young leaves are a favorite vegetable, or bark material for baskets, they have to be very careful not to say anything out loud about it. Remarking how good it looks, that it would be nice to have, or anything similar will bring repercussions from these spirits. Interpreting such remarks to mean that the speaker's spirit wants to guard and use that item, the minor spirit will reserve them for the speaker's spirit, and then cause him to sicken and die so that his spirit can return and care for the item.

A more violent example of this kind of danger reportedly happened to a friend a few years ago. He saw a tree near a waterfall which he wanted to use in construction. We were told that when he cut it down, the spirits pushed him off the cliff causing him serious injury. His leg was badly broken and he is still crippled. The tree itself almost landed on another companion. Our friend did not die because his relatives recognized the problem and, being of the Kulka clan with the pig totem, sacrificed a pig in honor of these spirits and saved his life.

The *coyapne neng* are spirits typically found in deep pools where two rivers meet, pools formed by water from narrow rocky gorges, or pools at the base of waterfalls. They can also leave these pools and live in a species of bamboo called *lai* or on exposed rocks or mountainsides but they do not live in or behind waterfalls. They steal people's spirits and hide them in invisibly fenced small holes in the jungle. Such stolen spirits are immature and so are "raised" as humans raise pigs. Sometimes little crying noises can be heard when walking through the jungle, and people then know that they are passing such an enclosure. The immature spirit remains in the hole covered by a flat rock at the base of a tree, in a cave, or other spirit house. The longer it remains there, the weaker and sicker its owner becomes until he finally dies.

Two other minor spirit types are the *giremban neng* and the *panpannya neng* who are male and wield axes called *eripo ya* and *galepo ya*. Their particular task is to assist Kain Dyen Ngop and Memeduman Ngop by felling trees. Kain Dyen Ngop sometimes gets strong winds (not spirits) from the *nandirip ati* and *nankwep ati* spirit houses and uses them to bend large trees in preparation for felling them onto people he wants to punish. The two spirit groups chop down the trees bent over by the winds. These spirits live near cliffs, in narrow river gorges whose rock walls almost meet, tall trees, narrow passes between mountain ridges, caves, pools, and swirling water or whirlpools.

There is also a set of female spirits in the form of banana trees. In the beginning Doyap planted several kinds of banana trees near the big ceremonial houses at Depeseban and Bopgon. Later Kwerepkor Ner's female child, *ungka ner*, bore daughters in the form of banana trees at these same locations. These banana tree daughters of Ungka Ner are important because people use this type of banana leaf to cover the ground at pig feasts before displaying and dividing the cooked pork. This usage is a way of recalling Ungka Ner, honoring her daughters, and indirectly honoring Kwerepkor Ner, Doyap's sister.

Another set of spirits is under the authority of the head spirit of the dead, Limdepunge. His subordinates inspect people who have been given sicknesses or have had their vital parts or spirits eaten by major spirits. When these minor spirits determine that the time is right, they deliver the death blow (*dena deiyo keca*). They also hasten death by performing "leavings sorcery" on people. They prepare the bundle of "leavings" (e.g., hair, fingernails, feces, food, or any other item closely associated with the intended victim) and leave it in a cave, pool, or hole so that the person will get sick and die. A general term for these spirits is *denbulung isok* 'those spirits who gather the dead'. Their names are *dening*, *potongyawa*, and *parumbuna*, meaning, 'death people', 'loss of hair', and 'gatherers of dead spirits', respectively. They live in caves, large trees, or on mountaintops.

There is a final category of beings about which little is known. Whether they are spirit or some subhuman race, they are the only type whose physical appearance is described. Nothing is known about their activities but they live on the edges of the universe to the north and west of Ketengban territory where the sky dome meets the earth. They look like people but they have tails like dogs or pigs. Those to the north are called *amubuna neng* and those to the west, *uyarkembop neng*.

Human Spirits: Spirits of the Dead

Like most Melanesian societies (Habel 1979), the Ketengban venerate their ancestors, both the recent dead and long dead. As noted in the section on Mankind, the soul of a living person is called *sambala*, but it becomes *isok sisa* 'true (evil) spirit' or *nimi isok* 'person's (evil) spirit' when freed at the person's death. The characteristic habitation of the spirits of the dead is on mountaintops, but they are so active that descriptions of them locate them in many other places. When residing on the mountain-tops, they live in ease and plenty. They marry and have children and have human-like social and political structures. The pool and waterfall spirits are the main ones to marry the spirits of the dead. Occasionally these spirits desire a living woman and, in order to marry her, cause her death. The spirits of dead men can take wives from the spirits already living on the mountaintops or remain single until a living woman they like dies. It is not possible to marry one's own spouse in spirit form.

The Ketengban do not distinguish between ancestors who have recently died and those who have been dead for some time. All are prone to be dangerous, although they may occasionally be benevolent. Their presence may be signalled by small sounds, breezes, and fireflies. Almost anyone may have dealings or encounters with the ancestral spirits, but specialists are usually more effective in such interaction than common people.

Though usually seen only by specialists, these spirit ancestors are fre-quently present among the living and participate in Ketengban social and ritual life. They are often interested in and help with the lives of their living relatives. They appreciate the display of traditional wealth at bride price exchanges or the display and offering of special foods and sacrifices in their honor and eat the essence of these foods via the aroma.

Even though a person is congenial and helpful in life, he or she may not be friendly and kindly disposed toward kin after death, and it is almost certain that he or she will be malevolent to nonrelatives. Though entreated to perform benevolent services on behalf of the living, the spirits of the dead are believed to be dangerous and unpredictable. Courting their favor may result in prosperity and health, and incurring their wrath may result in sickness, bad seasons, other calamity, or even death. These spirits are especially present in their own bones, some of which are kept in ritual houses or men's houses. Skulls are very powerful and at one time scores of them could be found in certain spirit houses. They were sometimes used as headrests, though not on a daily basis.

As the chart of the Ketengban spirit hierarchy (figure 5, p. 31) shows, the spirits of the dead are less powerful then the major female spirits and some minor spirits like Tau Pena or Nimi Dyen Bisam, but seem to be equivalent in power with most minor spirits and with human ritual specialists. They are more frequently active than most minor spirits and as equally active as human beings, primarily in connection with kin in their own area. They may be entreated to harm people farther away, being able to travel anywhere instantly. Unlike the major spirits, the spirits of the dead do not use the underground "hollow tree" tube system but travel through the air (*im nitamai*) or on the earth's surface (*tuai mutu*), and are sometimes visible to common people. The ancestral spirits do not assume any form other than the firefly. They do not possess or empower people but enter a person's body to eat the essence of that person's heart or soul. They do not enter animals but can cause sickness and death in pigs.

If someone has not maintained a good relationship with a relative, the spirit of the dead relative can cause the death of the living person or get other spirits of the dead or spirit beings to kill them. On the other hand, if a person had a good relationship with a relative, the spirit of the dead relative can argue in defense of the living person with other spirits bent on harming him and sometimes prevent his death. Quarrels over a human's fate can occur between all types of spirits, but no spirits can harm each other. They are said to be related by clan lines like humans.

The spirits of the dead have the power to steal a person's soul and take it into the jungle (just like the *coyapne neng* 'pool spirits' mentioned earlier) where they hide it in a hole, cave, or tree base and fence it in. These captured souls can be heard crying. If discovered early, this problem is treatable as described in the next section. When, however, the captured soul "matures" and is ready to make gardens like the ancestral spirits, the spirits of the dead report this to the major spirits who then "eat" the essence of the soul causing the still living, but sick, person's death.

The soul is released at death, but does not usually depart the body or *nimi gemna* 'person burial package' right away. After the initial three to four day period of grief and wailing, the body is wrapped in a certain type of tree bark. The spirit might take temporary trips during this period but always returns to the body. Then the body is put up on a small enclosed platform in a treetop or on scaffolding near a cliff face. It is essential that the place be near village houses (especially if the person was greatly loved or very prominent). The people can continually see the place and remember the person, and the dead person's spirit and the living have easy access to one another. Secondly, it is disrespectful and a sign of lack of affection to put the body far away from the house. Should relatives come from a distance to see the body and discover it has been placed too far away from the hamlet or not be able to see its face, they will be insulted and angry and might kill pigs and steal or kill women.

If the person was of no particular consequence or there is no danger of retaliation by relatives, the body might be placed farther away or in a jungle garden house. In the latter case, the walls, fire pit, and floor of the house are dismantled, and the body put on a platform just under or over the original roof.

Most frequently, the body is placed in a tree near the relatives' houses. Both the bark around the body and the wall of the enclosure in the tree have openings so that the dead person's face is visible. The body is placed in either a standing or sitting position, and the hole in front of the face is covered with bark cloth, which can be lifted for visual inspection by relatives coming from a distance to visit the body or for periodic inspections of the putrification process. This little window also allows observation of the final departure of the soul as it leaves to live as a person's (evil) spirit. These spirits are sometimes called *deneng* 'dead people'.

On the first night after the body has been placed on the scaffolding or in the tree, several brave men stand beside nearby houses and watch carefully for the final departure from the body of the person's evil spirit. The departure is signalled by the spirit taking the form of a bright fire-fly, (*mira*) falling from the eyes of the corpse. When the fire-fly falls, it is carefully watched to see where it will go. If it comes towards the house of the closest relatives, they attempt to catch it and throw it into the fire of the house. This action does not harm the spirit but prevents any person in that house from being "bitten" in the heart by the fire-fly, resulting in stomach sickness characterized by pain, sulphur burps, and heartburn. This stage of the sickness is treatable, but because those bitten are often people that the spirit senses are "ripe" for sickness and death, they usually die. If the fire-fly heads for another hamlet area, then someone will certainly die there soon. Those villagers can be warned if the watchers are so disposed. If the fire-fly flies in some other direction, then someone somewhere will die, but it will not be anyone nearby.

The spirits of the dead can also cause sickness and death in pigs. This might happen because the owner of the pigs had not properly or frequently honored the dead. It could also be revenge by a living relative via the services of the ancestral spirits for not having been given enough bride price. Perhaps the spirits themselves are angry at not having been given enough food gifts or sacrifices or by having their plans to kill someone counteracted by the rituals performed by another person.

The spirits of the dead do not usually take food from gardens, and there are no elaborate rituals for sharing a portion with them or leaving sacrifices to them in special places. However, whenever people are eating or feasting, it is important to think of these spirits and sometimes set food aside for them or bring some back to the house to put upon the shelf of Tau Pena to share with them. The important thing is not to anger the spirits by eating special food items out in the jungle without bringing some back to the house. When so angered, the spirits of the dead report to Tau Pena, who might report to Kain Dyen Ngop and get permission for the ancestral spirits to cause sickness or kill the offenders. Generally, as long as one honors these spirits by thinking of them and saying their names quietly while eating, they come quietly and partake of the food. If, at a feast, a portion of pork comes out of the cooking pit somewhat raw or if the pandanas sauce tastes bitter, it is because these spirits have eaten some of it. This cannot be prevented.

Sometimes people can entice the spirits of their dead relatives to punish people they quarrel with, especially for slights. For instance, if an older person feels that his junior relative has not been generous enough in sharing, he can ask ancestral spirits of his own or of that junior kinsman to kill the offender, his children, or his pigs. If done directly, the death is attributed to being hit with a spirit walking stick or arrow. These spirits can also kill by "leavings" sorcery or by asking the major spirits to do it. Such killing between kinsmen is called *wina* 'dividing or choosing', referring to dividing the affections (jealousy) and choosing which relatives to keep and which to dispose of for being a drain on the network of mutual obligations. It is difficult to sort out these events because the ancestral spirits often kill capriciously, whether or not the person has done anything bad, whereas the major spirits and Kain Dyen Ngop and Memeduman Ngop only kill for wrongful behavior.

The spirits of the dead may ask the major spirits or Kain Dyen Ngop to kill someone. In such a case, the person may go crazy and fall on a stake, desire illicit relations with women and get killed in the resulting trouble, get killed in battle, or fall from a tree. If the companion spirit or Kain Dyen Ngop or Memeduman Ngop initiates a killing, he can use ancestral spirits from any area under his jurisdiction. This particular kind of killing is often arranged by older women via their male kinsmen (or directly if she is a sorceress) because some junior man is not sharing generously enough with female relatives. The spirit men can arrange such killings via ancestral spirits, major spirits, or Kain Dyen Ngop. Once such a killing is requested, the clan of the person responsible for initiating it must be determined so that someone from that clan can try to intervene. Using the services of unrelated specialists is ineffective.

Another lethal method used by spirits of the dead is to slowly eat the essence of a healthy person's parts, weakening them until they are ready for one of the major spirits like Ketlingna Ner to eat the person's heart, causing death.

The Ketengban say that when the soul leaves the body and becomes a spirit, this is not the end of its developmental process. After a very long time, the spirit also dies and becomes a lower class of spirit called *parum*. The *parum* live near mountain peaks and high ridges and are not as active as *isok*. It is not possible to placate them with gifts and sacrifices since their names are not known. They do not travel frequently but when they descend from their ridgetops they kill people or have sexual relations with women, usually young unmarried women.

When the *parum* themselves finally "die" or become inactive, they take the form of petrified ironwood tree hearts and are called *ketamin co kola* 'heartwood of ironwood trees'. This is the essence of the dead spirit which, although inactive, is nonetheless dangerous for anyone but initiated men or spirit specialists to handle. These ironwood hearts are sometimes placed in spirit or ceremonial houses, especially if their shape is unusual or if they are "Y" poles. The outer layers of bark and softer wood which quickly rot and fall off the ironwood tree are thought to be the body (*talo tu* 'dirt') of the deceased spirits of the dead.

Rituals

This section gives an overview of the most important Ketengban traditional ceremonies and rituals and the rationale behind them. Like all Melanesians, traditional religion as practiced by the Ketengban is part of the warp and woof of their daily lives (Lawrence 1965). Theirs is an integrated holistic approach making few distinctions between sacred and secular. The system of rituals, both great and small, is so complex and extensive that this paper can do no more than touch the surface.[10]

For this paper, the term CEREMONY refers to those major events which are basic to ongoing life and prosperity, require the mobilization and participation of all the clans in a region, and are so extensive in their preparations and performance as to be possible only on a cycle of four to five years. There are two of these PRINCIPAL LIFE CEREMONIES: the *kwet* and the *youwa*.[11]

RITUALS, for purposes of this paper, are the almost endless variety and number of specialized practices which form most communication between

---

[10]Again it must be made clear that these ceremonies and rituals have largely disappeared among the Ketengban due to the acceptance of Christianity, but because the change is still in process they are presented in the present tense.

[11]When the Ketengban elders who used to be spirit specialists began to relate their view of past life and ritual practice, they emphasized that it was absolutely essential to understand these two ceremonies if the other ceremonies and rituals were to make sense. They said it was important to start with the *kwet* and the *youwa* ceremonies because if these two were not carried out precisely and regularly nothing else in life could operate as it should, catastrophic disaster would result, and probably all life on earth would cease to exist.

Ketengban men and the spirits. Rituals are on a smaller scale than ceremonies, may be carried out by relatively few people, may be the special province of a certain clan, and are usually performed as often as needed. Some of them are quite important and need to be precisely performed but do not involve large scale mobilization of people and resources. The two principal life ceremonies take months to complete, whereas rituals may be completed in a few days or even moments.

Categories of Rituals

For this paper, a classification of rituals is proposed for the sake of clarity. This scheme is not articulated by Ketengban people but is helpful in understanding the rituals. Again, they are but a sample of the ritualized actions which were commonly practiced by the Ketengban people, but which have now been almost entirely abandoned.

In the chart in figure 9, the two principal ceremonies are listed first, followed by rituals which are grouped according to three primary areas of concern: prosperity, protection or healing, and punishment or revenge.

Category	Name	Main Purpose	Performed by
Principal Life Ceremonies	*kwet deirina*	initiate young males	ritual specialists
	youwa	restrain major spirits "closing the holes"	ritual specialists
Prosperity	*kain yumna*	celebrate first fruits and prevent crop failure	ritual specialists
	dyen morona	heal crop failure	ritual specialists
	kain ouna	insure good sweet potato harvest	ritual specialists
	uyop dona	insure good general harvest	ritual specialists
	kwaning geikke lingna	insure large sweet potato harvests	ritual specialists
	am siringna	insure large taro tubers	ritual specialists
Protection or Healing	*loupla dona*	restore crops after major failure or rot due to breaking incest taboo	ritual specialists
	am kiringna	save lives threatened by spirit activity	initiated males
	yu dyena	repel a curse put on by a person	initiated males

(continued)

Category	Name	Main Purpose	Performed by
Protection or Healing (cont.)	dyen putana tep yangna	repel crop failure caused by pests	initiated males
	mi me pona	prevent infant deaths	any adult male
	nong kina	return lost soul to its owner	shamans
	isok mar gudona	remove spirits or spirit projectiles	shamans
	mi deipra talwalimna	protect initiates from pollution by newborns	shamans
	nimi popra yangna	protect against retribution or revenge killing	shamans
Punishment or Revenge	wina	cause death directly by spirits of the dead or their arrangements	initiated men or adult women
	mun dangna	ask major spirits to cause deaths	initiated men or adult women
	nimi gereng dona (nimi ker dona)	cause deaths by "leavings sorcery"	mostly women, some men
	me bungna pona (from lowlands)	cause a person's death	men or women
	baimar pona (lowlands)	cause a person's death	men or women
	wasban pona	cause a person's death	men or women
	merei deirina	cause a person's death	men or women
	bul dokotena	cause a person's death	men or women
	nimi bouse pona	cause a person's death	shamans
	gongona	cause a person's death	shamans
	nong kina	steal the soul of living persons	shamans
	deito dangna	return or steal the soul of living persons	shamans

Fig. 9. Rituals and ceremonies

It has been said that rituals indicate the aspects of life and the cosmic order about which people feel the most anxiety (Lawrence 1965), and this statement is true of the Ketengban. Knowing and mastering these rituals gives the Ketengban man assurance that though he does not control his world he can at least manipulate it by the rituals and ceremonies prescribed for him by Um Bo. Um Bo gave the necessary instructions for these rituals and ceremonies to the clan founders, and their practice is policed by his spirit, Kain Dyen Ngop. As mentioned, the spirits can only be entreated to help, not coerced. Although success is not guaranteed, ritual knowledge and practice portray truth and power and are the prerequisite for success in social, political, and economic arenas. The power exercised is derived from the deities which gave the rituals to the Ketengban and regulate their use. Ketengban men, from experience, expect that when the rituals are carried out properly they will work. Problems do occur, however, and Ketengban history provides many examples of something going amiss when a further ceremony or sacrifice is needed to bring about the intended results.

Ketengban concerns, revealed in their ritual and ceremonial life, are common to most Melanesian cultures and center on societal health and well-being and fertility of crops and animals (Lawrence 1965). The failure of crops is a major concern. The consequences to crops, if spirit veneration and rituals are not performed, are mentioned in connection with almost all rituals regardless of their primary purpose. The other most frequently mentioned danger is sickness and death, resulting from not honoring the spirits with special gifts and food portions. Maintaining good social relationships is important, since a person angered will often retaliate by calling on the spirits to bring about the death of the one who offended him. Also vital in maintaining life, proper relationships, and authority as shown in the mythology and ritual practice are certain rivers and mountains, key crops, animals (especially pigs), certain descent groups, and local clan associations.

Since Um Bo assigned most rituals to specified clans, carrying them out reinforces group relationships which might otherwise become unstable. The major ceremonies require much cooperation for acquiring and using the food and wealth necessary to the feasting, exchanges, and ritual worship. This cooperation strengthens group ties and consolidates intraclan identity as the clans perform the rituals and roles allotted to them by Um Bo as their exclusive rights, passed down patrilineally as a male heritage to first-born sons.

As in many Melanesian societies, Ketengban women are excluded from almost all major ceremonies and rituals (Lawrence 1965) and can only use a few spiritual techniques such as sympathetic magic and contagious sorcery or "leavings" sorcery. Among the Ketengban, women are regarded as greatly inferior to men and are physically and ritually dangerous to them. This same attitude is widespread among the peoples of Irian Jaya as well as those of Papua New Guinea (Lawrence 1965). Segregation from women is imperative during the performance of rituals, and women can be summarily killed if they learn about or happen on a ritual site and see what is taking place there. Careful adherence to taboos helps men to

retain sacred knowlege and succeed with rituals. These taboos are sometimes harsh and call for avoidance of women, certain places, certain foods
(especially "cold" foods), and water. However, there is no bloodletting or
beating as reported for other parts of Melanesia (Lawrence 1965).

Since the community as a whole needs each clan to play its assigned role
in ceremonial and ritual life, the Ketengban learn to maintain a large
network of mutually beneficial but competitive obligations with one
another, using bargaining, bribery, power plays, and placation in their
relationships. Their traditional religious life makes use of these same
strategies for coping with spirit relationships. Bribery, placation, coercion,
and even deception are part of their ritual interactions with the spirits.
Like other Melanesian societies, Ketengban ritual and ceremonial life
venerates the spirits of the dead by close proximity of corpses to the living,
extravagant mourning, food offerings, and male cult ceremonies which
include the dead (Habel 1979). They practice sympathetic magic, both
homoeopathic (or imitative) magic where "like creates like" and contagious
magic (or "leavings") sorcery. Examples of homeopathic magic include
using slimy bananas or eels to image and insure smooth births, or saying
the names of snakes with hundreds of ribs while planting a garden which
is desired to produce hundreds of tubers. An example of contagious magic
is to cause a person's death by means of his leftover food (which remains
in sympathetic contact with him). The leftover food is made into a bundle
which is either burned, sunk in the river, or put under a menstruating
woman's skirt.

The kwet and youwa ceremonies entreat favor from the great deities and
their regulative underlings by incantations, sacrifices, and passing on sacred
songs and knowledge. Although coercion is not possible, they try by incantations, invocations, and offerings to insure a specific result, often a reversal of
action attributed to a certain spirit. Though the spirits are not obliged to
benefit humans on the basis of these rituals, the Ketengban spend considerable time and resources to build the reciprocal relationships with spirits so
important in their human relationships. The spirits resemble humans in form,
emotions, and character. They reside and are active in man's world, though
they have supernatural powers and travel by extraordinary means. Elements
of the Ketengban sociopolitical and religious systems are characterized well by
Lawrence in his comments regarding the Ngaing of the Rai coast:

> The pragmatic quality of both [systems] of relationships is under-
> stood and expressed in roughly the same terms. A man fulfils his
> social obligations in order to make other persons with whom he

has human relationships "think on him" and fulfil their obligations towards him in their turn. Similarly, the aim of ritual is to make deities and spirits "think on" human beings and confer benefits on them. But the activities of gods and spirits in helping mankind have no mystical quality. They are believed to take place on the same plane of existence and are, therefore, just as real as those of human beings working together at any joint task. Thus although the Ngaing regard work in any important undertaking as a compound of secular and ritual techniques, they assume that both have the same validity. Both derive from the same source (the deities) and both involve co-operation between beings who inhabit the same geographical environment. [Lawrence 1972:218]

Principal Life Ceremonies

The two most important ceremonies are the *kwet deirina* 'putting the initiation' to initiate young men into the male pandanas cult, and the *youwa* in which the major spirits are returned to the invisible holes out of which they came. The Ketengban say this latter ceremony "closes the doors" on these necessary but dangerous spirits. The *youwa* ceremony coincides with the return of new initiates to their villages and normal life. Their reentry period is called *teru pangna* 'sprouting of branches', an appropriate metaphor as the new initiates come back to the village and add new members to the power base of men in the cult.

These two ceremonies, always performed in tandem, take about six months each to complete, and the preparation time for them is also around six months. Thus, the full ceremonial cycle takes approximately eighteen months. These periods are defined and regulated by the sun's position in rising and setting during the year or its northern and southern solstice (see figure 10). When the sun reaches its highest point in the southern sky, that is, the December solstice, then preparations for the ceremonies begin. These preparations continue during the time that the sun is descending to its lowest northern point, or the June solstice. At that time, the circuitous journey to the *kwet* initiation houses begins. At each of the eight to ten houses the same initiation ceremony is carried out. The sun, a living female spirit, is said to be weaving her net bag during this time while watching men on earth. Should she reach the uppermost point and the initiation ceremonies around the circuit not be finished, she might

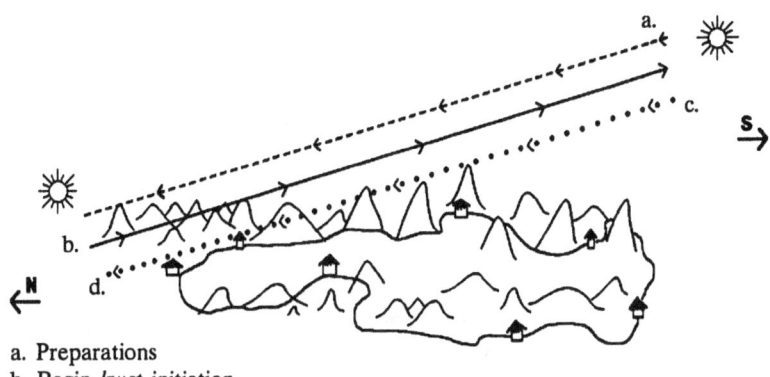

a. Preparations
b. Begin *kwet* initiation
c. Finish *kwet;* begin *youwa*
d. Return to normal life

Fig. 10. Diagram of main life ceremonial cycle

come down and put everyone into her bag, carry them off, and consume them, so it is imperative to keep watch and finish on time. By the time of the southern solstice all the initiations should have been completed, and the "closing of the doors" would begin. The *youwa* or *teru pangna* ceremony reverses the initiation path as the head spirit men make their way back around the circuit of spirit houses to "close the doors" on each house in turn, finishing at the starting point of Bopgon spirit house by the summer solstice.

The extensive preparations, number of people involved, time between groups of initiates, major commitments of resources and time, and the great importance of these two ceremonies precluded having them more often than every four to five years.[12]

*Initiation (*kwet deirina*)*

Preparation Phase. When the chief ritual specialists feel that certain criteria have been met and that it is nearly time to begin preparations for initiation, they secretly send out the word to all initiated men. The criteria are that sufficient pigs have been raised, enough boys have reached early

---

[12]These ceremonies having ceased, the time frame is estimated by the ages of those men who were initiation mates.

teen years, and the roofs of previous *kwet* houses have completely rotted away. Then, in utmost secrecy, preparations begin.

The actual time to start, at the sun's southern solstice, is calculated in the following way. Most of the villages in the Central dialect area (from which this data was gathered) are oriented in a north to south line. However, when looking at the whole area, they are found along an east to west axis in the valley systems on the north face of the eastern highland ridges. The rivers in each valley run from the higher southern elevations towards the lower northern elevations. Thus, when looking toward the rising sun from within those valleys, it appears that the sun is gradually climbing in the sky from its low point in the north to a high point toward the highest southern ridgetops.

The preparations begin secretly so that women and children do not realize what is going to happen. A time consuming task is to hunt, kill, and smoke enough of several types of cuscus needed for offerings and sacrifices. The most important of these is the *sakale* cuscus. Gardens must be planted to provide enough food for the feasting, especially certain species of sweet potato, taro, and sugar cane. Pigs must be arranged for, as well as certain kinds of net bags, body decorations, feathers, and special ceremonial items. These activities require a significant period of preparation time. All these items are taboo for noninitiates and women, and even speaking about them in front of noninitiates is forbidden.

One significant step in preparation is to choose a certain type of pig from the Midonban area and take it on the initiation circuit to the sites of the future initiation ceremonial houses. The pig is passed from man to man between certain key clansmen, and in each place fed for a period of weeks. The travels of this pig take several months and follow the route that Um Bo took (when dying in the form of a pig). It must stop and be fed in each location where Um Bo stopped, and each location then becomes the site of an initiation ceremonial house. The pig finally returns to the site of the first initiation in history at Bopgon at the westernmost Ketengban territory where a Dipur clan man gave Um Bo, in the form of the dead pig, to the elder of the Lepitalen clan.

This ceremonial pig is called the *molkaya* pig in the hearing of women, but the secret name *ore* pig is used with initiated men. This pig represents the essence of Um Bo who became a pig and allowed himself to be sacrificed to make possible the completion of the first initiation and the ongoing life of the people. The *ore* pig is always the first to be eaten at the beginning of the initiation cycle and is killed secretly at night and cooked. It is eaten first by the eldest Lepitalen clansman and then finished by members of that clan since they were charged with primary responsibility for the proper conducting of the *kwet* ceremonies. It was a Lepitalen man who had gone to find Um Bo in his pig form just before his death, and at that time Um Bo instructed him to symbolically kill him again and "eat him" by proxy or symbolically in the *ore* pig and so initiate men in perpetuity.

The *ore* pig also represents the other pigs subsequently killed during the ceremonial cycle. Um Bo instructed men to think of him when killing and eating this pig and other pigs and to take the grease from the pig's body and rub it on initiates' skins to restore them, so that they could become men and live well. Some of the fat and grease of the *ore* pig was set aside for use in each of the initiation locations. The parts of the *ore* pig which could not be consumed by the Lepitalen elder and his clansmen had to be buried the next day under the Bopgon house floor. This was the first initiation site, where the first spirit house poles were set, and the site of the house in which the Wisal, Dipur, and Lepitalen clan founders placed several items. They include Um Bo's pig jaw bone, the rope which bound him at his sacrifice, and the banana leaves from the pit in which his parts were cooked before they were eaten in a type of eucharistic feast. This all-important event in the mythology is reenacted in the eating of the *ore* pig, representing the essence of Um Bo, at the beginning of each *kwet* cycle.

Just as the location of the *kwet* house at Bopgon is established in the mythology, most of the other initiation houses find their roots there as well. Their names usually refer to a portion of Um Bo's body taken by the clan founders to divide and eat, or to something he did while dying as a pig. For example: *keraperban* is the location where Um Bo's *keram* 'kidneys' were taken; *malmokondam* is where Um Bo (as a suffering pig) got into a *mokon* 'pool' to cool off; *yanalip* is where his *yan tang* 'soles of his feet' were placed; *taramlyu* refers to the ceremonial house where his *taram yo* 'breast bone' was put. Um Bo's ribs and abdominal wall, *tapeka bol*, was deposited at another initiation location, *tapadam*. Um Bo's travail and subsequent consumption in the form of a pig by the earliest clan ancestors in these significant places make them legitimate locations for initiations into the male pandanas cult.

Another important preparation is building the *kwet* spirit houses. In each location, there are two main houses on a hilltop with a fence at the base of the hill, marking off the area as taboo for any noninitiates or women. The very tall fence made from closely woven poles can be built ahead of time and is one-to-two-hundred meters from the initiation houses at the top, making it impossible to accidentally stumble onto the initiation site. Passing through the single small entrance hole in this fence by any woman or noninitiate results in immediate brutal death.

One of the two large round houses on the hilltops is used for a preinitiation ritual and the other for the actual initiation, but there are also less important sleeping shelters for the neophytes during the months of instruction.

All the materials such as thatch, wood poles, mud for fire pits, and vines are gathered and put near the site for the ceremonial house. On the designated day, all the men who are to take part gather and build the entire building in one night by the light of handheld torches. It must be finished by morning so that no one can see the building process or the sacred things which are put in the house. During the building, the men are strictly forbidden to drink any water or to eat anything weak or cold such as snakes, frogs, or tadpoles. More importantly, they must be careful not to have any contact with women and continue to avoid any sexual contact with all women prior to and throughout the initiation period in their area. This avoidance also extends to food prepared by menstruating women, which might have contacted any surface possibly defiled by women's secretions. So women chosen to provide the men's food during these ceremonial periods are usually older sisters of the ritual specialists and they must prepare the food while on their knees. Sitting may defile the floor, and food can be inadvertently defiled if laid on the spot. Any physical contact or association with such food or water results in getting weak and soft just like those items. Further, this indiscretion angers Um Bo, resulting in famine and the death of people from starvation. The food which might continue to grow despite the curse would not be energizing or satisfying to anyone.

The headman for the ceremonial house in each area must sit and hold onto one of the four poles encircling the new fire pit during the building process. These four poles extend from the ground to the roof of every Ketengban house. During the process of tearing down the remains of the old ceremonial house and building the new structure, this man must sit holding the fire pole in the new ceremonial house without letting go, oblivious to any dirt or debris falling on him and not eating or drinking anything. The other men can have sugar cane to quench their thirst, but he cannot even have this until the house is finished. His job is to honor and stave off the major spirits by repeating their names quietly and gripping the pole. This homeopathic magic of gripping the pole where the spirits are often present is seen as gripping the spirits themselves. It is also to avoid misunderstandings by the spirits who may think that the men are going to tear down a key spirit house and not rebuild it. This is especially feared during the transition period before the new structure begins to take shape.

Partaking Phase. Once the fence and two houses are built, the initiation ceremonies can begin. The many novices are escorted to the fence around the taboo area with great fanfare by hundreds of initiated men. The sisters of the head ritual specialists for the area follow along behind the men and boys but put net bags over their heads to conceal their faces, allowing only enough sight to walk without stumbling. They keep their heads down as they walk but lift their hands and sing special chants and songs. Upon arriving at the fence, the men and boys go into the initiation site, but the women return to the village. Certain women may return to this fence periodically to leave food for those inside the taboo enclosure. Any woman later approaching the fence to leave food, however, must make shrill calls normally used in dancing to warn the men and initiates of her presence. If she accidentally meets a man wearing the special red paint, she must be put to death.

The headmen responsible for the initiation go into the first preparation house ahead of the new initiates. Inside, they stand side-by-side around the walls holding their bows and arrows. Key men from each clan then hold the purported severed forearm and hand of Um Bo which was given long ago to the Lepitalen man while he watched Um Bo's body being cut up. The forearm and hand which remained fresh forever, was bloody, and had long fingernails, is held in a certain way. One clan elder puts his hand palm up on the floor and all the other elders put their hands on top of his, one on the other, forming a tower of hands. Then Um Bo's severed hand is placed on top of their stacked hands. As each initiate is about to enter the preparation house, he must first take a bite or suck briefly on a large piece of taro which has a piece of smoked taboo *sakale* cuscus inserted in it. Eating the taro deposits a substance inside the initiate's body that protects him from having his soul eaten by the major spirits. In Ketengban mythology, this type of taro was given to children during the primordial era to keep them alive, and its essence remains in the end of the intestines to prevent spirits from eating the soul. The *sakale* cuscus is taboo to non-initiates and is a powerful representative of the major spirits.

After the boys have bitten or sucked the taro meat package, they enter the house, stepping lightly on the pile of elders' hands with Um Bo's hand on top. Then moving further into the house the boys form a tightly packed group around the fiercely burning fire pit. The men around the walls dance, chant, sing, pop their bow strings, and keep the boys in the center pressed close to the fire. The heat is to make the boys (and the men) sweat as much as possible to cleanse them of weak and cold fluids that would lessen their power and make them soft and weak. Loss of these weakening fluids also rids them of their previous power-draining associations with women and the food women and children eat such as birds, frogs, tadpoles, and snakes. Men participating in these intense ceremonial affairs must be made hard, hot, dry, and thus strong, by sweating away the fluids.

After the period of sweating, the men and boys proceed into the central *kwet* enclosure. There the initiated men of the pandanas cult again sing, snap their bowstrings, and dance around the initiates. This process is called *kwet warengna* 'hunting, looking out for the initiation' and it lasts all night. Sometimes the shouting and bow-snapping becomes so frantic and loud that the young boys faint from fear and exhaustion or soil themselves with urine, feces, or vomit.

During this night, the initiates must continually look at the sky, never at one another or at the ground so that they do not miss the arrival of the great spirit in the form of a snake-like piece of sugar cane. This event is called *sembela* (note the similarity to the term for soul or spirit, *sambala*). The boys watch for it intently all night, never certain when it may arrive. When it arrives (right over the gathered boys), they are supposed to jump up and attempt to grab the sugar cane and pull it down to earth where it will be torn to pieces as they all try to grasp it. The first boy to grab the sugar cane and pull it down from the sky will be greatly blessed. He will be a good, moral, prosperous, successful man, and people will listen to him and give him things. Such a high incentive makes the grabbing of the captured sugar cane frantic. Once on the ground, the cane is pulled out from under the feet of the boys by the men around them.

This *sembela* sugar cane called *ipikman gwei* or *mem gwei* can only be eaten by the head spirit men; if the new initiates eat it, they will be eating the source of their spiritual power and a substance rightfully only to be consumed by their spiritual elders and would be *mening keca* 'eating their own substance', something too closely related to their own spiritual power. (This same term is used in discussing incest). This action would result in losing their minds, or in doing antisocial things like not listening to elders, stealing, fighting relatives, and perhaps resulting in being killed.

The boys are also strictly forbidden to eat or drink anything from the time they take the taro meat sample into their mouths until the initiation ceremony is completed the next day. The initiated men, however, take turns going partway down the hill to feast on pig, cuscus, and sugar cane. If the novices eat food or drink water during the initiation process, they incur Um Bo's wrath and punishment on the people at large. At best the gardens will fail, and what does grow will not roast well but go to mush when cooked. At worst, the world will turn over and all people and living things be destroyed.

The *sembela* usually arrives just before dawn. On the morning after its arrival, the boys are led out of the initiation enclosure into the jungle where they are given their first drink which is sacred water from Limgonai, the habitation of Doyap, the creator. The water is in special gourds held in two hands by the spirit headmen who lift it to the lips of the boys one by one, giving them a drink while chanting *al me gwepne, limtai me gwepne*, 'I am dipping Al water, I am dipping water from Lim mountain'. Al refers to a pool which heals and restores life, just down the hill from a main spirit house location. Lim mountain was the original home and domain of Doyap and later Um Bo.

Cleansing and Teaching Phase. The new initiates next undergo a sort of baptismal cleansing. This takes place in a prepared pool where *ba* wood, the kind of wood that Um Bo had been tied to at his death, is used to dam up and deepen the water while incantations are said. Each boy is taken singly into the pool. While holding the boy's head in his hands, the head spirit man says some incantations, sings a song, and then immerses him in the water. When he comes out of the water, his body is scraped with the same kind of wood damming the pool to cleanse him from his childhood associations with women, consumption of weakening foods, and residence in women's houses. From this time on, the new initiates sleep in the men's house and avoid weak and cold foods unless incantations (*merye pena*) are said over them first.

After the baptismal cleansing, certain leaves having sacred mythological significance are used to wipe off their wet bodies. The boys are then led back to the initiation enclosure where they stand in the early morning sun to dry while incantations are said asking the spirit sun to dry them (endue them with power). After they are dry, the elders rub the boys' bodies with a mixture of rancid pig grease and bright red clay using several kinds of aromatic leaves. (The pig grease is from the body of Um Bo via the *ore* pig killed at the beginning of the preparation stage). In some areas a certain tree sap is mixed with the fat and red clay and put in the hair of the initiates which causes the hair to dry very hard and stiff. This striking red adornment is used thereafter for any special rituals or ceremonies throughout their lives. It is unclear whether the red color represents Um Bo's blood, pandanas, or something else, but there is no more important or admired color for the Ketengban, even today.

The boys remain outside until the sun has dried their red coating, then they go into the second initiation house to sleep but cannot lay down until one of the leading spirit men lays down first.

On the following morning, the boys have a regular bath in water and are again coated with the red grease mixture (*mure*). They then are taught a particularly sacred song recalling Um Bo's red ornamentation and specific type of net bag to remember and venerate him. This song can only be sung in the deep jungle where the largest hardwood trees grow, so it is called *yuan dam mut* 'near the ironwood tree song'. This is the first of many songs and chants that the boys are taught during their six months of seclusion for initiation. If women pass by an area and hear these songs from the jungle, they must call loudly and constantly in the shrill way they call pigs in order to cover the words of the songs because hearing them causes a gradual decline in health, resulting in death.

Sometimes a man who is suspicious that sorcerers caused his wife's death may climb a hill and begin to sing such songs out loud so that the women who performed the sorcery might hear these taboo songs and die. If an initiated man hears this singing, he will advise the relatives of the widower to try and stop him and quickly get him another wife to avoid calamity for everyone. A man singing such songs openly may invite his own death by doing so.

Closing Phase. After the novices stay in the initiation enclosure for approximately six months and the sun has again traveled to the low point in the northern sky, the closing feast and imminent return of the initiates to their villages is announced. At this time, people from all around the area are instructed to gather vegetables, cuscus, frogs, locusts, snakes, tadpoles, sugar cane, and other food items, many of which are not normally eaten by initiated males. Numerous pigs are also prepared. Late in the night, great pyres of wood with rocks on top are prepared and fired to heat the rocks for pit cooking the food after dawn.

Incantations are said as the food is put into the pits, recalling the secret names of Um Bo or Kain Dyen Ngop and finishing with the phrase *siktapkene, deipdongopkene* 'I am dropping you, I am putting you, Um Bo, into the pit'. Only initiated men participate in this feast and, while the food is cooking, they tear down the shelters where the new initiates slept during their seclusion. All the materials used are thrown over a cliff nearby so that later no one can see that the ceremonies have taken place. When the food is cooked, most of it is eaten immediately and the rest is taken back to the villages to share with initiated kinsmen who for some reason have not taken part. Any residue of bones, leaves, or wood is burned, and anything not totally burned, including the charcoal, is buried to camouflage any sign of the initiation.

Then the boys are taken to another hilltop nearby where black and red sacred drawings are made on trees with charcoal and red clay. These are to attract the powerful female spirits present during the initiation, who, thinking the drawings more interesting than the jungle in the direction of the villages, would want to stay there and not follow the men home. After showing the boys the directions to the ceremonial spirit centers to which they would come in future years, the head spirit men announce that all are returning home. The senior men shoot many arrows into the air at once over the boys' heads away from the direction they will take in leaving. This is intended to scare the female spirits and to drive them away in the opposite direction. Otherwise, they might follow the boys home and eat the spirits of villagers.

Reentry Phase. Word is sent ahead to the villages that the men and boys who have been absent for six months are on their way home. The people from the villages, including the elders and relatives of the boys, gather food and pigs for a feast and prepare a large pit along the trail on the return route. This great display of food is also to honor the malevolent female spirits, the spirits of dead ancestors, and Kain Dyen Ngop, who had been participating in the initiation ceremonies. Honoring them lavishly makes them happy and satisfies them, thus preventing them from following people back to their villages to eat the essence of people there.

An additional precaution is taken by building a tall fence across the main trail on which the new initiates would travel in returning to their home villages. This fence has only one hole in it through which the head spirit men and boys pass. Specific kinds of rotten wood, moss, water, and melted pig grease are mixed together and put in a large bark basket. As each man approaches the hole, he is sprinkled all over with this mixture squeezed from a moss sponge, then he steps into the bark container and passes through the fence. Certain *merye pena* incantations are said during this process which include major spirit names and phrases saying, "I am making your hands heavy and your feet heavy (paralyzed), I am turning your face away and closing your eyes." Then a mixture of rotten wood and cold water is sprinkled on their bodies causing the hot and powerful spirits to think of these men as cold. The spirits will not want to eat their essence because of this kind of sympathetic magic. The incantations are a combination of wish fullfillment and sacred invocations intended to prevent the spirits from following them home.

The hole in the fence is finally covered with certain banana leaves, and all the initiation leaders and the initiates go home, going first to the men's houses to eat any leftovers from the big feast that morning and sharing the food with any male (initiated) relatives not present earlier.

Renaming Phase. The initiates are given new names at a ritual where the head spirit men cook pandanas. While squeezing the oily red sauce from the steamed fruit, they take pieces of the inner membrane and give it to the boys while declaring their new names saying, "Your mothers and sisters have called you 'X', but now your name is 'Y'". Upon eating the pandanas membrane *kain tang*, the new name becomes official. The names are previously chosen by each boy's male relatives in consultation with the spirit headmen. The final step of the boys' reentry into normal village routine is to reintroduce them to their mothers using their new names.

The fathers of the boys had already ordered certain kinds of cuscus to be killed and smoked in preparation for this event. The smoked meat is tied to each boy's right arm and he is taken by a shaman to his mother's house as his mother waits inside. A hole has been cut high in the wall opposite the house door and approaching it on the outside the shaman lifts the boy's right arm and inserts it through the hole, announcing the boy's new name. The mother lightly shakes his hand, takes the cuscus meat with fire tongs, and eats some of it. The shaman and boy then return to the men's house, eat taboo portions of a sacrificial pig, and go to sleep.

The next day the shaman and the boy return to the mother's house with small pieces of meat and some fat from the sacrificial pig. This time they enter by the door, and the mother and other female relatives move around the wall out of the way. The fat and meat are waved while incantations are said, indicating that these items represent the essence of Um Bo and Kain Dyen Ngop. This ritual honors the spirits and assuages any anger at the boy for now associating with women, eating food prepared by women, or eating food put on the floor where women might have sat. Though during the *kwet* ceremonies the initiates have been forbidden to have anything to do with women, their houses or their kinds of food, the rules have now been revised upon their reentry into village life. This waiving ritual informs Um Bo and Kain Dyen Ngop that, although the rules have changed, the boy will only do these things if the proper incantations are said beforehand.

Closing of the Holes (youwa)

The *youwa* ceremony must take place immediately after the initiation and training period and serves to insure that the major female spirits who lent their power and participated in the initiation activities are now satisfied, with proper veneration bestowed upon them and will now return to their holes underground. As explained earlier, these malevolent spirits can travel from place to place in an instant via a tunnel system of hollow trees underground. Most terminals of this system are invisible holes near the main ceremonial and ritual houses. Since the spirits come from those holes in order to go to empower the initiations, they now must be induced to return to the holes. The invisible doors to the holes need to be closed to prevent the spirits from roaming and looking for men's souls to eat. Therefore, the shamans revisit each spirit house during the next six months, feasting in the spirits' honor and inviting them back into their holes so that the doors can be shut.

The second purpose of the *youwa* ceremony is to placate the enormous man-eating spirit pig *nimi dyen bisam* or *mukup ati bisam*, who is always looking for people to eat. This spirit pig is ready and waiting just underground near the *youwa* houses and needs to be kept from opening his huge mouth and devouring everyone.

The third purpose of the ceremony is to insure a good harvest. A special spirit garden (*mem wa*) is planted and the *youwa* ceremony provided with sacred raw materials for planting other gardens in the coming year.

The *youwa* ceremony, described only briefly here, lasts only four to five days, but the preparation and waiting time between stages takes several months. The ceremonies are done for the whole area in an overlapping fashion, not one after another serially. Pigs, taboo cuscus, sugar cane, various decorations, and feathers must be gathered for the extensive feasting to honor the spirits. Then the *youwa* house must be rebuilt on the traditional site after the old remains are cleared away.

Only men from designated clans can collect the sago fronds and wood for the *youwa* houses since they are representative of Um Bo's hair, beard, and eyelashes. Specific guardian spirits of these materials must be appeased, and only certain clans like the Kwace, Kulka, and Mitne have the authority to do so. When the men come bringing these materials, people meet them on the trail with partially cooked, bloody meat so that the spirits think the people are so anxious to honor them that they do not even have time to properly cook the meat. The red color also pleases the spirits.

The actual house construction takes place in much the same fashion as that for the initiation houses: at night, in secrecy, with two Bidoman clansmen sitting patiently on each side of a spirit pole in the house with their index fingers pressed on opposite sides of the pole. They do this during both the building process and the four-to-five-day feasting and ceremony. The pole is an ironwood tree heart thought to have been planted by Um Bo in the beginning. Building at night prevents noninitiates from seeing this highly sacred pole.

When the house is built, the taboo cuscus and pigs are secretly killed and feasted on, but no water is drunk; sugar cane is used to quench thirst.

After two or three days, a second stage ritual is performed. The ritual specialists and shamans instruct the other men to gather at a designated spring on a hillside or cliff. On that day the spring has mysteriously dried up. The men squat in a semi-circle in front of the dry spring in anticipation. The Kulka ritual specialist responsible for this ceremony holds a specific kind of water gourd in his hands and taps it at the mouth of the spring while chanting incantations.

After a time the assembled company hears the first rumblings and gurgling of moving water, and suddenly the water spurts from the spring with such force that it sprays the assembly of men. The water comes out carrying many powerful sacred objects to be used in future rituals, especially those related to garden fertility. These items include bits of stone, hardwood, bone, cowrie shells, and fossils. Some are only visible to the shamans, so they collect these and give them to the headman responsible for the ritual who then distributes them to others. All these items are then stored on the wall opposite the entrance in the special sacred place in men's houses and have power to promote garden fertility and healing.

These aids to man purportedly spurt from the nostrils and penis of the man-eating spirit pig. This is evidenced by the forceful way they came from the spring and because secret names of the spirit pig are in the incantations chanted while the gourd is held in front of the spring.

On the last day of this second stage, a spirit garden is cleared and planted. Sacred items are buried with the potato shoots and incantations are said, indicating that the garden is in honor of the spirits. A large tree is left standing in the middle of this garden plot with its limbs cut off. Young men climb it and working down from the top paint black and red designs all over the tree. The spirits, pleased by these interesting designs in their honor, are distracted from normal gardens where they might steal or ruin the harvest.

Then the men wait for several weeks until the taboo garden (*mem wa*) needs weeding and the roof of the *youwa* house begins to show need of repair. Again, special animals, pigs, and other food are collected for another two-day feast, and the spirit garden is weeded. On the third day of this feast, the prohibition against water is lifted. On the fourth day a pandanas feast is held, and the ritual to close the holes of the spirits is performed.

Rock outcroppings serve as steps at the doorway of many of these spirit houses. These have been worn smooth and rounded by years of use. They are thought to represent the snout of the man-eating pig, Nimi Dyen Bisam, and are the place where he and other spirits emerge from the ground. The ritual specialist takes some designated pork and fat and, saying incantations to keep the spirit pig happily underground, partially burns some of it to make a strong odor. This meat and fat is repeatedly rubbed on the rocks, and incantations are chanted to please the spirits so that they will be induced to stay there and not follow the people to their villages. More of this meat and fat is rubbed on or burnt on a flat rock which is ritually turned over to cover the invisible hole from which the spirits came, thus closing their door to the world of common men.

After this ritual is performed at each initiation site and at the designated *youwa* house shutting all the "doors," it is felt that the major spirits are safely at rest unless something else arouses their anger.

Prosperity Ritual (*dyen morona*)

Most Ketengban ritual categories have a myriad of specific rituals and detail. Those listed in the chart at the beginning of this section are simply representative, and only one prosperity ritual is described here.

Most prosperity rituals are invocations for bringing fruitfulness of crops or livestock, but the *dyen morona* 'asking for food' is particularly interesting. It is similar to the *kain ouna* and the *uyop dona* prosperity rituals, but is distinctive in that it employs manipulation. The *dyen morona* ritual, carried out with great seriousness to deal with crop destruction by pests, is an enormous ruse designed to fool Kain Dyen Ngop. Perhaps this ruse is thought possible because it is his distant presence in the eastern territory (where he is generally referred to as Memeduman Ngop), which is being addressed. Memeduman Ngop, being associated with the people and territory of the east, is not a benevolent figure to people of the central and western areas. This ritual takes considerable effort and mobilization of people and resources; in the practical Melanesian way (Lawrence 1965:7), everything has specific reasons and purposes. Here the purpose is to follow Um Bo's specific instructions in order to halt or avert crop or livestock failure.

When small marsupials that feed on tuber crops flourish and multiply, they dig up the gardens and eat or destroy the tubers along with the vines. Pandanas can be damaged and mutilated by parrots, and owls destroy breadfruit. This calamity is thought to be caused by Memeduman Ngop and his sister, a female spirit variously called *nupsemsemkor ner* and *memeberberkor ner*, who are angered when men from the central area take wives from the east, particularly from different tribes. When the children of Memeduman Ngop and Memeberberkor Ner are removed from their jurisdiction by intermarriage, it causes a reduction in the gifts given to them. They then in anger send the marsupials, birds, and rodents to eat the crops and cause famine. The famine takes place in the home areas of the offending husbands.

The strategy for stopping the destruction and insuring plentiful harvests is to perform a masquerade to make Memeduman Ngop believe they not only intend to send back the eastern women, but also that most of the population from the affected area will go with them. The area left bereft of people is then of no interest to the spirits, and Memeduman Ngop believes he is gaining new people to honor him in the east.

When pests start destroying crops, the people go to the village where someone has married 'a woman from the east' *(memeduman nere)* and reminds everyone of the danger that Memeduman Ngop and Memeberberkor Ner will bring huge net bags, fill them with the food from their gardens, and take it away. Furthermore, they may then bear additional spirit children who will cause deaths and crop failure in the area. Then everyone present in that village, with great noise and commotion, begins to collect things in their net bags as if to make a major move. They take all of their valuables—stone axes, special feast foods, fire tongs, chickens, etc. These full nets are given to the eastern women or those associated with them, who put them on their heads as if prepared to leave. Other people pound on walls, pour water on hearth fires, throw things out of the houses, uproot small bushes and trees and throw them about, and generally make a commotion demonstrating their definite rejection of and final departure from the area. Small children, old people, and others not participating in the ritual quickly and quietly hide under debris or on a trail until everyone has left the village. They are forbidden to start fires or indicate their presence in any way. Any sign of valuables or people remaining in the village will make Memeduman Ngop realize he is being duped.

Just before the procession leaves the village, the head spirit men take bloody pork and wave it over the people's heads. This is done because the spirits like red, and like a dog following a person dangling a tasty morsel, the spirits will follow the group away from the village, eager to eat the pork sacrifice. The heavily laden people then set off down the trail toward the east, to a place near the eastern border. There is constant announcing of the departure and pounding and shouting along the trail to show they are starting life anew in a distant location.

When the travelers reach the place near the border, they encounter a high fence across the trail with a small door cut in it, which has been recently prepared for their arrival. Everyone loudly announces that since they are almost into the eastern or Memeduman area, they will stop, rest, and have a feast in the spirits' honor. The special feast food which has been prepared beforehand and carried in the nets is produced, and a feast held. Some of the spirit headmen go through the fence and paint red and black designs on the eastern side. The spirits, having followed through the fence door, will be interested in the area on the side of the fence markings and not care to return back through the fence. Many gifts and sacrifices are left hanging on the eastern side of the fence to placate and entice the spirits to remain there. As an additional ploy, they rub the scent gland of the *sakale* cuscus on a flat rock, turn it over and, while saying incantations, place it with the scented side down on the ground by the door on the eastern side of the fence. The spirit is attracted by the aroma and enticed to return underground by the scented rock being turned over.

Afterwards, they sleep on the western side, and early in the morning men station themselves all about the area. With their stone axes, they cut many medium-sized trees almost through. The scent gland of a taboo cuscus is heated in the fire to release a strong odor and then is rubbed on an arrowhead belonging to the head ritual specialist. He then waves it over the heads of other men who stand with their bows drawn ready to shoot. Then, at a given signal and with great shouting, all the trees prepared earlier are felled at once, and the arrows are simultaneously shot into the air in an easterly direction. The spirits follow the enticing scent of the taboo cuscus on the first arrow along the trajectory of all the arrows into the east.

During this commotion, everyone else runs into the jungle away from the main trails as fast as possible and from there they secretly make their way back to the previously abandoned village. The cumulative effect of all these actions is sufficient to dupe Memeduman Ngop and Memeberberkor Ner into thinking that everyone has moved to the east under their jurisdiction. This action is sure to stop crop destruction and insure plentiful future harvests.

Protection or Healing Rituals

Six rituals from the protection and healing category are discussed below: the *kulmana kwetena* for preventing sudden death, *am kiringna* for healing adult illness, *nong kina* for returning a lost soul, *isok mar dorona* for removing spirits or spirit projectiles, *mi me pona* for protecting newborns from soul-eating spirits, and *yal kouna* for insuring long life for a newborn.

*Protection against Sudden Death (*kulmana kwetena*)*

The phrase *kulmana kwetena* 'healing the thunder' refers to the fact that the thunder is a sign that, having incurred Kain Dyen Ngop's anger, someone is about to be suddenly and violently killed. The person might have killed someone Kain Dyen Ngop did not want killed or eaten food in a selfish and arrogant way, not honoring to the spirits. In the latter case, he may have secretly eaten something such as pork, pandanas, or large taro which was noticeably large and special, without honoring Kain Dyen Ngop or bringing some to share in the men's house with others or offering some to Tau Pena. This action is especially bad since everyone can see that a particularly large or notable item of food is gone and knows the proper procedure has not been followed.

Kain Dyen Ngop, learning of the transgression, sends for the *ibe* or *sanipe* spirit who, like his cassowary namesake makes a loud explosive sound when angry. The spirit makes the noise by snapping his bowstring, as evidenced by a great clap of thunder. All the men instantly recognize thunder as a signal of death, and someone knowing the appropriate incantations to avert this is quickly called.

The remedy is sympathetic magic of the homeopathic and contagious types. If the thunder is very loud, then the ritual specialist takes a rock and wipes sweat from the guilty person's armpit on it, then places it near the firepit poles and presses down on it while chanting incantations like: "I am smoothing down your ruffled feathers, I am pressing your bow to the ground, I am detaching the string from your bow." Alternatively, the names of certain long snakes thought to be spirit snakes are spoken while the specialist says, "I am breaking your many ribs so you are limp, not rigid, I am smashing your head, go back to your place." Then the rock is tossed out into the rain where the heat from fire and armpit will be cooled and so, by association, the anger of the spirit.

If the thunder is not so loud, then the incantations are said soothingly while stroking sweat from the specialist's armpit onto the firepit poles from top to bottom. By association, this act is smoothing down the raised feathers of the cassowary or the hair of the man-eating spirit pig which may have been called to eat the person. In this case, the rubbing is analogous to rubbing a pig's stomach which calms him so that he lays on his side as any domestic pig is known to do.

Scraping the Taro (am kiringna)

This ritual can be performed by the shamans or the ritual specialists and is effective in healing certain sicknesses or preventing a person's death if he has offended a spirit. Besides sickness, one sign of such an offense is that the sacrificial food and tobacco put on Tau Pena's shelf or left hanging in a net up in the rafters is not accepted by the designated spirit.

This rejection can only be discerned by the shamans. Four or five days after the offering is made, the shaman inspects it to determine if the spirits have eaten it and been satisfied. If not, death is sure to follow unless the ritual of *am kiringa* 'scraping the taro' is performed.

The shaman bakes a large taro tuber (*am*) in the fire. After taking it from the coals, he wipes the sweat from his armpits on it, and then scrapes off the ashes and outer layers with a bamboo knife. The scrapings fall on the head, neck, and shoulders of the sick or endangered person while the shaman or specialist says incantations using the names of the indicated spirits and stating the desired results, as "You are going to be solid and hard like an ironwood tree. You are going to be hot and firm like this taro. You will not be sickly and die nor will your children."

Then the ritual specialist turns his back on the victim but faces the Tau Pena shelf. He holds the taro in his hands behind his back, and the victim eats from it while the ritual specialist announces to the spirits that the man named has killed pigs and made offerings in addition to the ones which were rejected. Further, the man in question is planning to offer more pigs and pandanas, proving that he is a good person. This offering demonstrates that he is the treasured possession (*mauwa*) of the ritual specialist and, by extension, the spirit and should therefore be spared.

The ritual specialist then gives the taro to the man who eats most of it and shares the rest with other men and his children who are also in danger. Pork or pandanas offered to the spirits in connection with this ritual is shared among these same people and with the specialist. During this period, no water (cold, weak) can be drunk because it will weaken the effectiveness (heat) of the magic.

Returning a Lost Soul (nong kina)

The *nong kina* 'putting (it) into the body' ritual serves to combat the perpetual danger of having a person's soul stolen and hidden in the jungle or on mountaintops by a major spirit or the spirits of the dead. If the proper offerings of pork and pandanas are made, and if the shaman has a good relationship with Kain Dyen Ngop at the time, then help is possible. Kain Dyen Ngop tells the shaman where to find these hidden souls. The shaman goes and, upon hearing the whining of the stranded souls, finds the flat rocks which mark and close the hole where the souls are being kept. These rocks are identifiable by the fingernail scratches underneath made by the souls trying to get out. The shaman then captures the soul, invisible to normal men, wraps it and the rock in dried pandanas leaf fibers, and puts it in a net bag. Holding it with both hands, the shaman brings it to the victim's men's house where all men can hear the soul's mewling.

This bag is placed on the victim's chest, who holds it with both hands while the shaman completes the ritual by saying incantations with the names of the indicated spirits, invocations that the person might live, and naming the measures taken to incapacitate and banish the spirits. After a time, a *yeri bo* leaf which has a red back recalling the blood sacrifice of Um Bo, is waved in circles over the victim's head. The shaman then jumps up and runs around in the house, pounding on and grabbing at the walls as if to catch an insect, eventually catching the invisible lightning bug (*mira*) or the 'eye' of the victim's spirit. This flying away of the *mira* causes dizziness and blurred vision in sick people.

A hissing sound emanates from the hands of the shaman holding the *mira*, and he places it on the victim's head at the site of an infant's fontanel. The shaman then blows softly on this spot while saying spirit names and incantations, telling the soul to return to its owner. Then a piece of string is tied around a bit of hair over the spot to "close the door" where the soul might again escape. This string should not be removed but must rot or fall off by itself as a sign that the soul is solidly in place and the person will live.

Removing Spirits or Spirit Projectiles *(isok mar gudona)*

The final healing ritual to be described is very common and has endless variations for specific symptoms and sicknesses. The *isok mar gudona* 'pulling out the spirit arrow' ritual is to repel a spirit who is eating a person's heart, stomach, or soul, or to remove a spirit arrow which has been shot into a person's body by a major spirit or by the shaman on the orders of the major spirits.

The spirits feeding on a person's soul are often the female *ketlingna ner* or *yami ner*. Their removal involves using *wedina*, which may be either a piece of fat and skin from a sacrificial pig or the scent gland of the sacred *sakale* or *tau pena* cuscus which has been smoked and long kept on the shelf for sacred objects.

The shaman puts this bit of meat or fat on a stick and heats it until it smells strongly. Then, chanting incantations and speaking spirit names and ancestral names, he waves this over the victim's head with the red-backed *yeri bo* leaves. The sight and smell pleases the spirits, recalling past sacrifices and gifts made to them and deflects their interest from the person to the eating of these favorite *wedina* foods. The shaman also takes *sukolonga* 'grease-soaked banana leaves' from pit-cooking the sacrificial pig and rubs it along the victim's body and stomach. Then, with a quick gripping and jerking motion, he "pulls out" the spirit and throws it out the door. Finally, some water (wet and cold) might be thrown out the door to chase away the spirit. Each kind of spirit makes a characteristic sound when leaving a person: spirits of the dead make guttural sounds; the *sakale* or *tau pena* cuscus spirits make growling sounds like a small dog; *ketlingna ner* and *yami ner* make clicking sounds accompanied by short yelps, gasping, or crying.

These same procedures are also frequently used in removing spirit arrows or other projectiles from people. Having removed them, the shaman then lays these items, such as sharp bones, rocks, and hard wood splinters on a banana leaf for display. Not all are deadly, but all of them cause sharp stabbing pains until removed.

Preventing Death of Newborns (mi me pona)

Soul-eating spirits are particularly likely to attack newborns, being attracted by the smell of the vernix and blood on their bodies. Newborns are never washed lest the water carry their scent to the spirits, who will then track the infant and kill it or steal its soul. As Anne Sims reports in the next article of this volume, there are many rituals to prevent or overcome spirit problems for newborns.

The name of this ritual, *mi me pona* 'killing children (by) water', refers to the baby's scent carried by water in various ways, attracting the spirits. If rain or water splashes on the child near a river, the smell is borne by the frogs, eels, tadpoles, or small water insects to the habitation of the spirits. The water carrying the blood might contact tree or plant roots dangling in the river which carry the scent to the spirits. Similarly, ants perform this same function for the spirits on dry ground, carrying the scent and transmitting news of the baby to the spirits who then come to kill it.

To prevent this eventuality, the husband or maternal male relatives prepare a number of small packages of various fragrant leaves over which incantations have been said. These leaf packages are put in the house and in net bags in which the child is carried to suppress the scent. Whenever the mother travels out of the village, she drops these packages on the trail at key points in the areas she frequents, stepping on them to crush the leaves and release the fragrance, thus masking the scent of her child from searching spirits. Laying the child on these leaves in the carrying net also masks the newborn scent and protects the baby as the mother travels about.

This ritual is unusual because women have a direct participating role in performing it. The packages can be prepared by a ritual specialist or by any initiated man but, once made and thrown from a distance to the door of the woman's house (men cannot approach the house or child for a long time to avoid pollution), the job is the mother's. Women understand only a minimum about the ritual, but know that it is essential.

Protecting the Life of an Infant (yal kouna)

The *yal kouna* 'planting a shoot' ritual is to protect the life of a child and is for mothers who have had several stillbirths or infant deaths. Again the mother plays an initial role since men carefully avoid menstrual pollution. The remainder of the ritual, however, especially the incantations, is performed by men.

After the birth, but before the umbilical cord is cut, the mother takes a bamboo knife and severs the infant's little finger at the second joint. The severed portion is wrapped in leaves and handed to the helper woman who carries it with fire tongs and gives it to a man knowing the *merye pena* incantations. Careful not to touch it, the man buries it in a garden hole and plants either *teiyong* 'an edible leafy vegetable' or *tawanye* 'type of banana' over it. Both of these plants have extensive tangled root systems which are very difficult to uproot and continually put out new shoots for many years, i.e., they are both tenacious and self-propagating. The homeopathic and contagious magic imparts the characteristics of the plants to the infant by way of its finger, to encapsulate and protect it from danger by association with the root system and to give long healthy life by association with the self-rejuvenation of the new banana shoots coming up.

A similar process is employed to prevent a child's death and to insure the birth of further children, especially males. The proper incantations are said near a boy's house, and a branched taro shoot (*kwa am yal*) is planted there because it produces multiple branched tubers. This is to protect the boy and insure that more boys will be born.

Near a newborn girl's house, incantations are said and a sugar cane taro which does not produce a tuber but only edible leaves is planted. This

indicates a preference for male children since no tubers are produced.
However, the girl's life is protected since sugarcane taro is the favorite
food of the infant-eating spirit *daiyankar ner* 'she-will-come-from-Dai-
mountain woman'. This plant is particularly plentiful in the Daibalal river
valley where Um Bo sent many of the first women to live and has always
been traditional food for females. Daiyankar Ner sees this plant in her
honor and eats it instead of the female infant (Anne Sims, this volume).

Punishment or Revenge Rituals

As figure 9 (pp. 60–61) shows, there are many different rituals in the
punishment category. Only one subcategory, the *nimi ker dona* or *nimi
gereng dona,* is clearly contagious magic of the "leavings" type with an
almost endless variety of methods, but all are typical of those well docu-
mented throughout Melanesia.

Any initiated male who knows the incantations can do this type of
sorcery, or a ritual specialist or shaman can be asked to do it. Counteract-
ing such sorcery has to be done by spirit mediators, shamans, a clansman
associated with the particular spirit (if known), or most effectively, the
person responsible for the curse. Punishment rituals are unique in that
some of the practitioners are old women. These women are greatly feared,
not because their magic is more powerful but because they are believed to
be more vindictive, easily offended, and less predictable.

The rituals follow familiar patterns. Something from the presence of or
having close association with a person such as left-over food, nail parings,
hair, feces, or some small personal possession, is secretly collected. The
sorcerer usually packages the "leavings" in leaves or a green bamboo tube
and then does something to it which is effectively transmitted to the victim
because the item remains in sympathetic association with them.

The sorcerer basically determines what sort of death the victim will
suffer by what he does to these packages. If the bamboo tube is burned in
the fire or crushed between rocks, the death will probably be sudden and
violent. If the package is left to rot in the jungle and be eaten by insects
or hung in a remote tree or "drowned" in the river, then the death might
be slow and painful.

If someone realizes that *nimi ker dona* has been worked on his relative,
a shaman might find the packaged leavings in time because Kain Dyen
Ngop will sometimes tell shamans where these packages are by subtly

glancing in their direction while traveling with the shaman. The shaman can then indicate by a show of fingers to the relatives, the size and number of the packages and thus how many pigs or pandanas are needed for the healing ritual. Occasionally the package might be found in the sorcerer's house or on their person. One such sorceress concealed the leavings package under her skirt next to her vagina, exposing the victim by contagion to her vaginal secretions and menstrual blood which would result in a wasting disease and death. Such vicious sorcery could be punished by immediate death for the practitioner at the hands of the victim's relatives, and in this particular case, the relatives responded in this way.

The rituals listed in figure 9 are some of the ones available to the Ketengban who want to cause harm to others or their possessions. Sorcery can be directed at humans, livestock, or gardens. Sometimes relatives of the target person are killed, and even the sorcerer's close relatives are not exempt if they are offensive. For instance, one ritual uses a cattail-like vegetable (*bakke*) to cause trouble for the sorcerer's own married daughter because the groom's clan has not paid enough bride price or the bride's mother has not been getting what she considers to be her fair share of bride exchange items. This kind of *bakke*, covered with fine red nettle-like hairs, is struck on the fire poles in the young bride's house and rubbed over the floor where she sits and on her nets. The names of female spirits such as *ketlingna ner* are said along with incantations specifying desired results. The fine red hairs on the vegetable represent the pubic hairs of the spirit effecting the punishment. The stinging quality is important because it makes the girl restless in her house. She will not sleep well, will not stay in one place, and will be unhappy working until she either runs away to her mother's village or becomes promiscuous. Any of this behavior can cause her, her husband, and his clansmen serious trouble and possibly even death.

Conclusion

The Ketengban people have complicated and intricate procedures for dealing with supernatural beings who are both numerous and malevolent. The paragraphs above have sought to describe for the reader the basic beliefs and rituals that relate to these procedures.

References

Flannery, Wendy. 1979. Appreciating Melanesian myths. In Norman C. Habel (ed.), Powers, plumes and piglets: Phenomena in Melanesian religion, 161–172. Bedford Park, South Australia: The Australian Association for the Study of Religions.

Habel, Norman C., ed. 1979. Powers, plumes and piglets: Phenomena in Melanesian religion. Bedford Park, South Australia: The Australian Association for the Study of Religions.

Heeschen, Volker. 1978. The Mek languages of Irian Jaya with special reference to the Eipo language. Irian 7(2) June 1978. Abepura, Irian Jaya, Indonesia: Universitas Cenderawasih.

Hogbin, H. Ian. 1948. Pagan religion in a New Guinea village. Oceania 18:120–45. Reprinted in John Middleton (ed.), 1967, Gods and rituals: Readings in religious beliefs and practices. Austin: University of Texas Press.

Lawrence, Peter. 1965. The Ngaing of the Rai coast. In Peter Lawrence and M. J. Meggitt (eds.), Gods, ghosts, and men in Melanesia: Some religions of Australian New Guinea and the New Hebrides. London: Oxford University Press.

Lévi-Strauss, Claude. 1963. Structural anthropology. New York: Basic Books.

Sims, Andrew. 1986. Ketengban kinship. Irian 14:14–41.

Sims, Anne. 1992. Ketengban childbirth practices. This volume.

Voorhoeve, C. L. 1975. Languages of Irian Jaya: Checklist preliminary classification, language maps, wordlists. Pacific Linguistics Series B.31. Australian National University.

Myth and Metaphor in Ketengban Pregnancy and Childbirth Practices

Anne Sims

Contents

Myth and Metaphor in Ketengban Pregnancy and Childbirth Practices

Many of the beliefs and practices of the Ketengban in regard to pregnancy and childbirth are rooted in Ketengban mythology.[1] Consider, for example, the following account of creation:

> At one time all of creation existed on a mountain top called Limgonai. Doyap [the principal cultural hero and creator] wanted to see this life spread farther beyond the area of Limgonai so he dispersed it from the mountaintop. The two main rivers, the Bime and the Tanime, also had their origins here. These rivers, which were like living beings, had been gradually building in a common pool behind dams. They competed with each other to see which would break out first. Finally, as Doyap was sending everything off the mountain, the Bime River simultaneously burst forth and, rushing down the mountainside, carried with it the best of all that was created—people, animals, and plant-life. It filled up the large valley system that is now known as the Bime area and started to flow out through the gorge at the lower end. There it spread out

[1]Data for this paper were gathered primarily during July 1989. Thanks go to the many Ketengban women who willingly shared information concerning this area of their lives with me, with special appreciation to Nia Duyala, Tena Megouke, Yosopina Meku, Dorong Wisal, Sukrop Lepitalen, and Eprenes Wisal. I would also like to thank Yohana Steinbring for her translation of the Schiefenhovel article. The data gathered by my husband, Andrew, from the Ketengban men and his very helpful insights are also appreciated.

into the lowlands. Um Bo [the other main cultural hero who was responsible for disseminating instructions concerning how to live] saw this and was distressed by it. He knew that if this happened everything would be too widely dispersed and would become diluted and therefore weakened. He wanted all of this life to thrive and remain concentrated, so he took his knife, which was a piece of hardwood sharpened on both edges, and inserted it across the gorge to stop the waterflow.

The analogy between creation and birth is compelling: the valley filled with water and, bearing in it all that is living and fertile, is symbolic of the child in the abdomen. The small gorge opening at the lower end of the valley represents the birth canal. In the same way that a child is born in the breaking out of amniotic waters, so all living and created things were originally carried into the world in the rushing water of the Bime River.

Many Ketengban customs regarding pregnancy and childbirth are rooted in and validated by their mythology and their metaphors. In the paragraphs which follow, I describe details of such practices and beliefs.

The last fifteen years have been marked by a great deal of social change. The Ketengban have not been particularly averse to new ideas from the outside and indeed in many instances have welcomed them. The changes that have come about have affected all areas of life, including pregnancy and childbirth. For this reason, I have tried to describe this life process as it occurred both in former times (by use of the past tense) and as it occurs in the present day (by use of the present tense). One of the most noticeable differences in the present is the marked absence of rituals and ceremonies involving the veneration and appeasement of spirits. These practices were primarily carried out in hopes of achieving positive outcomes and avoiding calamity in the various aspects of bearing children. Another change is the diminishing concern by men regarding pollution from vaginal blood and secretions, a common preoccupation in Melanesian cultures (Faithhorn 1976:87).

Although pregnancy and childbirth practices are fairly uniform throughout the Ketengban area, it should be noted that there are some variations among the three major dialect areas—referred to simply as Eastern, Central, and Western. The information for this paper was gathered in Omban, one of the eight larger villages located in the Central dialect. For the sake of consistency and because of incomplete information from the other two dialects, this discussion is primarily concerned with the Central dialect area residents.

In regard to present day practices, I would also like to note that Omban is one of the villages that has undergone the most social change. More isolated areas, even within the Central dialect, may not have experienced change to the same degree.

Menstruation

For the Ketengban, as in many Papuan cultures, liquids carried the connotation of coldness, softness, and weakness. Blood lost by women either through menstruation or birthing, as well as other vaginal secretions, were viewed by men as particularly dangerous pollutants. For this reason special care was taken to avoid contaminating men with these liquids, through either direct or indirect contact. These precautions were especially important during the period surrounding the carrying out of rituals and ceremonies, including male initiation, and during war.

In the past, there were special menstruation houses that were referred to by several different terms: *bari ati, samai ati, yuan ati,* and *yailyati,* though the first was the most commonly used name. Although these houses were used as dwellings for menstruating women, the women were not restricted to them for the entire time. They were free to go about some of their daily routines such as gathering firewood and feeding pigs. If a woman saw men approaching on the trail, though, she was obliged to call out a warning to them that she was a menstruating woman. The men would then take a different path to avoid contact with her. She also could not cook food for men during this time. It was feared that the food which was to be consumed by the men might inadvertantly come in contact with the floor, her skirt, or her hands which in turn were likely to have been polluted by her secretions.

A girl's first menstrual period was referred to as *samkweria* and succeeding ones as *bari ati.* Older women today report that there were no special ceremonies or equivalents of male initiation rites for girls. Only after she was pregnant would they explain to her about childbirth.

It was desirable for a girl to be married before or shortly after her regular cycle of periods began. If not, there was fear of attempted intercourse by a spirit. Since girls could be betrothed while still quite small, at times they would go to live with the future husband's mother (*nin*) or clan sister (*mal ner*) from about seven or eight years of age until they were old enough to begin living with their husbands. This arrangement could begin before regular menses was established.

In the process of change over the last fifteen years, these restrictions have been lifted. Today women stay in their own houses, sitting on leaves when the flow is heaviest, and are free to go about their daily routines. There does not appear to remain any inordinate concern about their preparing food for men or sharing their dwelling space.

Pregnancy

Pregnancy is believed to occur following frequent intercourse. According to the Ketengban, intercourse must take place daily for a period of several weeks in order for conception to occur. As expected, the first sign of pregnancy to a Ketengban woman is the cessation of the menstrual period. The lethargy and nausea that are commonly experienced are believed to be the result of the woman's blood pooling in her abdomen to form the baby. A fetus is thought to receive nourishment by tilting its face up and opening its mouth to catch food as it drops to the mother's stomach while she is eating. This belief also accounts for the meconium present after birth, which is thought to be the feces resulting from food ingested by the unborn infant. The placenta is believed to be a protective cushion for the child while *in utero*.

Now, as in the past, there are no work restrictions per se for a pregnant woman. She carries on her daily routine as much as she feels like doing so. If tired or ill, she just stays home for the day or does less work.

In the past there were a number of foods that were considered taboo for women in general, whether or not they were pregnant. These foods had been designated by the Ketengban hero, Um Bo, as ones to be eaten in his honor, and portions of these were to be left for him and other spirits as sacrificial gifts. Only initiated men were allowed to eat these foods. The list included the following:

kain	'red pandanus'
tarkai, doup	'species of bananas'
dimitan, wauwam	'species of taro'
bikme gwei	'type of sugarcane'
makar, sumid	'species of *sayur lilin*'
mai	'type of green leafy plant'
kapang tu	'all species of cuscus'
bisam tu	'most parts of the pig'

Other than these food taboos for all women, in general there have never been any additional food restrictions during pregnancy. Several women have commented that if there is any one food that tends to nauseate one more than any other during the first trimester, it is manioc (tapioca).

Sexual relations during pregnancy are not prohibited but depend on the preference of the couple. However, women may sometimes be reluctant to have sexual relations for fear the unborn child's skin will be damaged.

Prior to Conception

In the past a special ritual called *garangna alen* or *potong kepmana* was performed for newlywed girls. The ritual was carried out before pregnancy in order to ensure that she and her husband would be prolific. The husband, along with his male relatives, killed a number of cuscus (a kind of marsupial) and gathered them together with netbags, axes, and other trade goods. The male go-between who had originally requested the bride's hand for the husband arranged with her parents the time for the ritual to take place. When the time came, the go-between took a live cuscus from the husband and hung it around the wife's neck in a net bag. The bride went to the doorway of her mother's house and, while still standing outside, leaned forward into the doorway. Her mother would greet her without looking at her and say, "Oh, have you had a boy or a girl?" She would then take the net bag off over the girl's head and put it on the floor. After killing the cuscus which was inside, she took its kidneys and liver and cooked and ate them while the girl was still standing in the doorway. Not until this was done would the girl be invited into the house. When the rest of the animal had been cooked, the bride's mother, father, brothers, and other designated male kinsmen would eat it.

The primary purpose of this ritual was to appease two major spirits called *ketlingna ner* and *yami ner*. These female spirits posed the greatest danger for women and children. The kidneys and liver of the marsupial, which represent the hearts of people, were eaten by the mother in honor of and by proxy for these two spirits. This act was taken in hopes of satisfying them and diverting them from eating the hearts of the bride and her future children. On this occasion, time could not be taken to cut up and cook the whole cuscus for to do so might make these two spirits impatient. They might just decide to forget about the cuscus and eat the heart of the new bride.

Although this ritual was usually carried out for newlyweds before any children were born to the couple, it could also be performed for a woman whose children consistently died. In this case, it was said that the spirits responsible for the children's deaths were hard to satisfy; they expected more food offerings to be given. Therefore, this same ritual was carried out in order to appease them.

The mother of the bride played one of the primary roles in the *garangna alen* ritual. However, if she was displeased with her daughter, her son-in-law, or his family, she could be the catalyst for trying to bring about some calamity in their lives. The type of situation that might provoke her to such action would be shameful behavior on her daughter's part, such as extramarital sexual relations. An inadequate brideprice (in the mother's eyes) paid by her son-in-law and his male relatives might also incur her anger. This sorcery was known as *wina* and although often set in motion by the mother of the bride, it was ultimately carried out by men. The mother would complain, and any kinsman who could be classified as her brother or grandfather could call on spirits to whom they had access by virtue of their clan membership to bring about misfortune in the couple's lives. For example, the young bride might subsequently be barren or all her children die. Another possible result could be that she or her male kinsmen who had not been sufficiently generous with the brideprice would be murdered.

In the case of an inadequate brideprice, the spell could be reversed by the same men who had cast it, if at a later time sufficient brideprice was paid. This further payment would need to be accompanied by feasting and dancing hosted by the kinsmen of the husband. The bones of the marsupials that were eaten at these feasts were placed in a pile as they accumulated and then thrown into the fire all together. The men would pronounce a spell (*merya*) by saying, "Just as I've thrown many bones in the fire, the girl will have many children."

Birthing House

Sometime during a woman's pregnancy, a birthing house was built if one did not already exist for her hamlet. This was a separate structure from the menstruation houses. While these houses were not far away, they were always situated downstream and lower than the village itself so that odors or anything that might be contaminated with blood would always be carried away from the village by wind, rain, or river water.

Husband's Role

The building of the birthing house could be arranged by the husband, but he could not take any part in the construction of it. For him to do any hard labor, such as driving support poles into the earth, stomping the wet clay down for the firepit, or wrapping and tightening vines, could result in the baby's passage being obstructed later during birth. Similarly, while his wife was actually in labor, he avoided this same type of work or any actions that might be analogous to tightening or shutting off the birth canal. Conversely, he would often loosen his rattan waistband and the bindings on his axe in hopes of facilitating the delivery.

Another symbolic precaution of this nature was taken by the husband prior to the child's birth. Several times throughout a woman's pregnancy, especially towards the end of it, the husband might come up beside his wife while she was sitting or lying in the hut, and surreptitiously slide the string of her skirt down with his toe while saying quietly or silently, "Um Bo, I'm taking your knife out. I'm opening the way."

This statement refers to the creation myth mentioned in the beginning of this paper. It is symbolic in the sense of removing the obstruction that prevents life from flowing out, being born with the passage of water. It also is a means of venerating or appealing to Um Bo, perhaps the most important cultural hero. Showing allegiance to him and doing things in the way which he prescribed reduce the risk of interference in the birth by malevolent spirits, since they, too, are in many respects subject to him.

The husband could also be helpful in a practical way by placing some food and firewood in the birthing house just prior to his wife's entering it.

Miscarriage

Miscarriages are referred to as *kain parana*. This is the Ketengban term for the process by which pandanas leaves (*kain*) bundle themselves up and start forming a fruit which soon rots and drips out the bottom. The analogy to a miscarriage is obvious. The pandanas is normally formed and comes to solid maturity within the enfolding fronds of the palm which then finally open and release the fruit. Sometimes, however, the pandanus dies and rots inside, resulting in draining liquids, and so it is with a human miscarriage. What should have been a viable infant, formed to maturity in the womb, for some reason dies and is lost in a flow of blood.

The Ketengban are not really sure what causes a miscarriage. In the past, the explanation in some cases was that a spirit had entered the woman's stomach and squeezed the baby to death. Initiated men (*kwet neng*) did not go anywhere near these women for several weeks for fear of contamination. To prevent further miscarriages, the *garangna alen* ritual described above was sometimes performed.

Women today are much less likely to suspect spirit involvement in miscarriages and most say they are not sure what the cause is other than the possibility of working too hard in the early months of pregnancy.

Labor

Banana Ritual

Between the time a woman feels the first twinges of labor pain but before she goes to the birthing house, her husband again makes an attempt to ensure a safe, speedy delivery for his wife. To do so, he and a few other men bake, peel, and give her *tawanye* bananas. As they give them to her they repeat over and over the *merya*, or spell which includes the words, *dumdum, dulyoma, tauwa*. The recited words are the names of several species of eels and catfish from the lowlands area. The banana skin recalls the slipperiness of these eels and fish. The names recited and the bananas eaten are to aid the baby's wet, smooth body in slipping out, utilizing a type of homeopathic magic (Ryan 1972:1003).

The significance of using a *tawanye* banana is that it was the original banana species that came down from Limgonai mountain during the dispersion of created things and became the first and most important staple for the people. It is said that sometime in the distant past, in the primordial era, children were kept alive by feeding them *tawanye* bananas during a famine. Thus the associative symbolism is a dual one: slippery items for smooth delivery, and a staple that has been considered to be life sustaining from the earliest known era. (See the section on stillborn prevention ritual under Birth below.)

Drinking Water Ritual

In the past, once labor had begun, the woman left the village and proceeded to the birthing house. She also began a total abstinence from drinking water that lasted until several days after the birth. This practice is referred to as *me tu tandyena*. If this taboo was transgressed, it was thought that several calamities involving rain would befall the child in his later life. For example, on days of special ceremony involving feasting, dancing, brideprice payment, and the like, it would rain until the next morning resulting in everyone returning to their homes unsatisfied and feeling as if they had come for nothing. Another such problem resulting from such a transgression was that on garden clearing days it would rain and the work could not be finished. Similarly, hunting trips would be rained out, leaving everyone involved miserable and with nothing to eat. To avoid all these potential future problems, it was crucial that the woman not drink water.

Participants

Women Assistants. Among the Ketengban there are no women who are considered to be midwives either by virtue of special training or experience. In the past, more often than not, a woman delivered alone, but there could also be one or two helping women (*melimna nerepe*) assisting her with the birth. The *melimna nerepe* could be any close friend or female kinsmen. The overriding concern was to protect the men, particularly the recent initiates, from any immediate contact with the delivery. Keeping the number of women involved and all of their paraphernalia to a minimum proportionately reduced this risk to the men. If a woman really wanted to serve as a *melimna nerepe* to a friend or relative who was delivering, she left all extra food, net bags, and grass skirts in the village and went to the birthing house with only the essentials.

The birthing houses used in the past no longer exist today. For the most part women give birth in their own houses in the village or, if labor begins while in the garden or jungle, they may also give birth in an outside house (*bura ati*), which is a small jungle house. If alone in the jungle or at night, a woman may still give birth without any assistance.

Nowadays, a woman is usually assisted by one or two women who are either relatives or close friends. Although they often sit around chatting with one another, when their services are not needed at that moment their purpose is to be quietly supportive of the mother, getting whatever she may require.

Other Participants. Since the taboos about women's blood only exist in vestigial form today, men, including husbands, may be present and on rare occasions even assist with the birth. Children can be present, but smaller children are usually taken off by the father or another woman or girl. Older ones usually play outside with friends. Often other people drop by the house to see how the labor is progressing. How many actually come into the house or stay around is generally determined by the woman in labor. Some prefer more privacy while others do not seem to be bothered by the presence of those who are not involved. The women who assist her (*melimna nerepe*) are usually sensitive to this need and "run interference" for her. A closed door indicates a wish for privacy. If the labor is particularly long or difficult, many people may gather around the house. I observed on one occasion a large crowd gathered outside a house in the middle of the night. Bonfires were burning, people were chatting, and women were weaving netbags. They were there out of curiosity and although concerned about their friend, a light-hearted atmosphere prevailed.

As labor progresses, the *melimna nerepe* gather leaves to place under the woman during delivery. Banana leaves are first placed on the floor of the house and on top of these are laid various kinds of green and dried leaves (*balteng bo, minkong bo*).

Positions and Procedures during Labor

During labor the woman stays around her house, but often, especially if the labor is prolonged, takes walks outside in the vicinity of the village. As she feels a contraction coming, she grabs hold of the rafters of the house, the fireplace poles, or the hands of one or two people. Gripping one or the other of these items, she hangs on remaining in a squatting position until the contraction passes.

It is forbidden to lie down or to sit with the legs together during labor or delivery. There is the belief that if the mother is in a prone position, the baby will become confused and try to come up the throat. This belief is not unreasonable in that there is no concept of the baby being contained in the uterus which has only one opening at the cervix. Rather, the baby is seen to be in the abdominal area but not otherwise contained in any kind of enclosure. Both the aperture in the throat and mouth and that at the vagina are thought to be open to the baby, being more or less a continuous track through the body.

Though commonly used in treating pain and sickness, the use of nettles in childbirth is discouraged, but not strictly adhered to. Many Ketengban believe that using nettles could result in the child being born with sores or a rash similar to that caused by rubbing nettles on the skin.

Labor pains of greater intensity in the back indicate that the child will be a boy and labor pains of greater intensity in the front, a girl. Other than this indication, the Ketengban feel there is no way to predict the sex of the child.

Complications

If there are complications in birth, a "wait and see" attitude is usually adopted rather than taking any overt action. If the baby is long in coming, one possible explanation is that blood has pooled at the cervix making it difficult for the baby to pass through. In such a case, a person can come behind the mother and put their arms around her with hands meeting over the top of the uterus. Gentle pressure is applied to assist in expelling the baby. If an arm or leg presents first, the danger to both mother and child is recognized and again they wait it out rather than trying to manipulate the appendage or body of the infant.

Birth

As the time for the delivery approaches, the woman squats or kneels over the leaves that have been put down for her. In the past she would also call out that the birth was about to take place. All initiated males (*kwet neng*) who were within hearing of such a warning would run off, fall on their faces on the ground, and cover their faces and ears with their hands. This was done to shut out the infant's first cries and the birthing smells. To have heard these cries or to have smelled these odors was believed to result in severed intestines and death.

Cutting the Cord and Disposing of the Placenta

After birth the women wait until the placenta is delivered before cutting the umbilical cord. In the case of a retained placenta, the women are reluctant to cut the cord. They fear that the cord will go back up into the mother's body preventing the placenta from delivering at all. They are concerned that this action would result in a serious infection and possibly even the mother's death.

In the past, after tying off the cord with a piece of natural fiber, the cutting was always done by the mother. This was accomplished with a strip of razor-sharp bamboo, called *pa*. Although *pa* is still the most commonly used instrument today, it is more often one of the female helpers who does the cutting rather than the mother. The cutting of the cord should be done with a downward motion because it is believed that to cut with an upward motion causes the baby to urinate during its infancy in a long, high stream, while a downward motion causes the urine to fall. After being severed, the cord is given no special cleaning or other care.

In the past, the mother was the only one to dispose of the placenta. Either wrapping it up in the leaves on which she had given birth or just carrying it in her hands, she placed the bundle in the fork of a tree (if possible) overhanging a cliff. This mode of disposal was to prevent contamination of either people or domesticated animals. If such was not possible, it would be put off in a remote area of the jungle. So great are these concerns with birth contamination that among the neighboring Eipomek women, even the mothers themselves must avoid touching either placenta or baby until the vernix has been wiped off (Schiefenhovel and Eipo n.d.:128).

In present day practice, the attending women help wrap the placenta in the leaves on which the baby was born and put down fresh ones for the mother. They then take the bundle away, burying the placenta and discarding the leaves at the edge of the village.

Although the people are not as concerned as they were fifteen to twenty years ago, there are still negative connotations associated with female blood and fluids. Care is taken to avoid contact with the blood, and the women assisting are careful to wash their hands well. Any blood that has gotten on the woven floor of the house is washed off. If any falls through the floor to the ground beneath the house, the dirt there is turned over and water poured on it. It is still believed that if any animals, such as chickens, dogs, or cats, ingest the blood, they will become sick and die.

Deformities and Deafness

In the past, deafness and some deformities were believed to be the result of the mother's indirect contact with a *cuscus*. All species of these small marsupials were taboo to women. If her husband had, for example, either eaten one and then had intercourse with his wife or if he had brought some of the meat even to the porch of the house and she had inadvertently smelled it, the spirits would be angered and retaliate against the child.

Crippled or deformed limbs are still thought to be the result of the baby being in an odd position as it is forming within the tight confines of the mother's stomach. Again, although it was not specifically mentioned by people interviewed, based on other traditional beliefs about miscarriages and birth defects, it can be presumed that in the past spirits were also thought to be involved in this misfortune. Arm and leg presentations were definitely seen to be caused by malevolent spirits.

Complications

Death of Child. In former times if a child was stillborn or died soon after birth, the mother herself disposed of the body by placing it in the fork of tree branches as was done for the placenta. Alternatively, it could be placed in a cave or in the roof area of a jungle house (*bura ati*). The house would then have its lower walls removed and be abandoned.

Death of Mother. If a woman died while in the birthing house, other women would take the body outside and carefully lay it on some leaves prepared for that purpose. From there men would come and, using the leaves so as not to touch her, lift her body onto a length of bark. It was crucial that they not actually touch her with their own bare skin. Once the body was wrapped and tied up in the bark, it was disposed of by placing it in a cave or throwing it off a cliff.

If the baby survived, the helping woman (*melimna nerepe*) or some other woman (if no one had helped) would take the child and care for it. If the baby later died, it was presumed that the dead mother missed her child and had come back to reclaim it.

In present practice the handling and burials of both stillborn babies and women who die in childbirth are no different from those of anyone else who dies.

Infanticide

As in many other Papuan groups, infanticide was practiced among the Ketengban in past decades. One of the primary reasons for infanticide seems to have been a wife's desire to take revenge on her husband. The aggravating offense on his part might be that he was not providing enough materially for her in the way of garden land or pigs, that he was treating her harshly, or that the bride price (*ner tappa*) had not been large enough in the first place. She might also try to punish her husband out of jealousy over a second wife.

Female infanticide might also be urged by the husband. His wishes, however, were not always followed. At most times in a woman's life, she was subject to rules and regulations dictated by the men and the spirits. During this one period of time, though, while she was alone in the birthing house, she was in a sense more the master of her own fate and that of her child than at any other time. If she chose to do away with her child, that was her prerogative. Furthermore, if she was alone, no one else need necessarily know. She could let it be known that she had killed the child or simply claim that it was stillborn.

The mother alone was the one to dispose of the child, and it only occurred in the birthing house. This result was obtained either by not cutting the umbilical cord and simply leaving the child until it died or by more aggressive action. Two reported methods of the latter sort were either striking the child repeatedly with a piece of firewood or stuffing the mouth full of rocks until it choked to death.

In recent years the only case of attempted infanticide that we know of occurred in the village of Omban. In this case a woman became pregnant by a man other than her husband. Shortly before the baby was born, her husband informed her that he wanted her to kill the child when it was born. Other people reported him saying, "The baby is not mine and I do not want to hear it crying in this house." She delivered the baby alone at night by herself, cut the umbilical cord, wrapped the baby in leaves and placed it in the outhouse. People found the child the next morning and it was cared for by women from her own clan. However, the baby died when about six weeks old. (There were several women taking partial responsibility for the child but no one taking primary responsiblity, so the child probably died of accidental neglect.) The prevailing sentiment in the village, which was fairly strong, was that what the woman had done was really wrong. Although the women caring for the child were concerned for its welfare, there was resentment expressed by them towards the mother for having shirked her responsiblity and surprise that she was apparently lacking in maternal instinct.

Sex of the Child

Since the Ketengban are a patrilineal, patrilocal, and male dominant society, it appears that the preference in the past was for male children. Parents today accept a child of either sex. Generally no comment is made that would indicate feelings about the matter. On occasion, though, I have heard a mother express pleasure at having a daughter who will grow up to help her in the garden and with the pigs, even if only on a temporary basis until she is married. Others have commented that a male child will eventually become a hunting partner of his father and a help to him in heavy work when the father is older.

Twins

When asked today, the Ketengban say that twins have always been accepted and seen as neither a blessing nor a curse. They are not really sure what causes multiple births. In the past it was taboo to refer to twins as forked children (*kwa nyape*) as they are called today. Rather, children the same age (*amsu nyape*) was the term openly used. Even though informants say there was never any danger from spirits in connection with this word taboo, in every other case of name or other specific word taboos of this kind, the fear of reprisal from spirits is a prominent factor. Secondly, given the somewhat unusual nature of multiple births and the fact that other events or objects not readily explainable were attributed to spirit activity, it would seem anomalous for this circumstance to avoid such an interpretation.[2]

Stillborn Prevention Ritual

If a woman had given birth to one or more children who were stillborn, or who died shortly after birth, upon the delivery of her next child the *yale kouna* ritual was performed in order to protect the life of this child and that of any succeeding children. Immediately after the birth, before the umbilical cord was cut, the mother would sever the little finger of the baby's right hand at the second joint. The severed finger would then be wrapped and carried with tongs by the woman assisting in the delivery to the village. There it was taken

---

[2]There is one set of twins at least thirty years of age that we know personally. One is male and the other female. In light of female infanticide in Ketengban culture and the common practice of infanticide in regard to twins in many cultures throughout the world, this seems significant to me.

with another pair of tongs by either a man or a woman and buried in a hole made in the ground with a stick. On top of this spot, as incantations were said, one of two types of plants—either a *teiyong* jungle green or a *tawanye* banana—were planted. The roots of both of these plants are very extensive and both put out profuse numbers of additional shoots for many years. The belief was that just as the root system would over time tightly encircle and enclose the severed finger in the package, the life of the child would be protected. Further, just as these plants regenerate themselves, putting out fresh growth continually, it was hoped that the child would enjoy a long and prosperous life. Again, this is an example of sympathetic magic of both the homeopathic and contagious types (Ryan 1972:1003). In the former case, the characteristics of the plants will be reflected in the child's life. In the latter case, long life for the child is insured because the finger, remaining in sympathetic contact with the child though physically removed, is efficacious in transmitting these benefits to him.

The choice of these plants also bears cultural significance regarding two of the primary female spirits *yami ner* and *limbali ner*. The jungle green is covered with fuzzy hairs which were thought to represent the pubic hairs of *yami ner*, a female spirit. The second female spirit, *limbali ner* also has life-giving attributes. Not long after the world was created there was a partial famine. The only remaining food was the *tawanye* banana. The *limbali ner* spirit, feeling pity for the small children, chewed some of this banana up and fed it to them thereby contributing to the ongoing life of mankind via these early children. By venerating her in this way and by using that same substance which sustained life during an earlier crisis, assistance is sought for ensuring the life of this child.

The *yale kouna* ritual was also understood to be predictive in nature. If the plant dried up, it was believed that the child would die before reaching adulthood. If the plant thrived, then the parents could assume that their child would also thrive and they could go about planning for it with every expectation of a long and happy life.

Postpartum

Care of the Child

Birth residue. In the past it was forbidden to bathe a newborn. The vernix, blood, and other fluids from the birth plus any dirt that adhered to the child were left on it. All of this residue collectively was referred to as *mi kawa*. If the baby were to be bathed or to come into any contact with water, bits of the *mi kawa* would fall to the ground and possibly be carried off by ants to various places which were inhabited by spirits, primarily *ketlingna ner* and *pontiana ner*.[3] The spirits might pick up the scent of the child from these fragments and come to eat it or to woo its spirit away. A child whose spirit was being approached in this way by one of these spirits would become ill with malaria (*yoni pu*), languish, and eventually die. For this reason also women could only eat unwashed potatoes. They would brush the dirt off with their feet, bake them in the fire, then peel the skin off, and eat them.

Because of possible contamination with women's blood through the *mi kawa*, men were not allowed to touch or be near newborns. If a man did come into such contact, he would become ill with *mi deirir tal walimna* or *mema tal walimna*. These sicknesses were characterized by stomach and intestinal pains, eventually resulting in severed intestines and death. No man could be around a child until it was three months of age. After this time ritual specialists (*mem neng*) and initiated men (*kwet neng*) could be in contact with them. For noninitiates (*noupet neng*) the time span was six months because they were younger and their spirits considered weaker. Once the whitish appearance of a newborn (*mi kulkul*) had disappeared and the baby's skin had become noticeably darker, any male could be around the child.

As an extra precaution against possible contamination of a man through the *mi kawa*, a woman could not carry sweet potatoes in a net bag near the child. The potatoes were carried instead in a bag in her hands in front of her, with the child in a net bag on her back. After three to six months, however, she would reverse the arrangement carrying the child in front and the potatoes behind her.

Fathers today still do not show much of an interest in their infant children either by giving affection to them or talking about them. Women contend that the men are this way because they consider the care of

---

[3]*pontiana* would appear to be associated with the word *pontianak* used by some of the language groups on the north coast of Irian Jaya to refer to the spirit of a woman who dies while pregnant. The prevalent idea in those groups is that a *pontianak* spirit is considered extremely dangerous and is thought to eat the livers of living people. Since she is endowed with the ability to fly, eggs are placed in the armpits of the corpse, and needles are put under her fingernails to prevent her from flying around in search of victims.

infants to be woman's work. But, in fact, the men seem to be embarrassed if the subject is broached. Considering the taboos of the past, it is perhaps not surprising that this kind of social response should persist. In a general way, Ketengban people felt that calling special attention to a new child in any way could result in the spirits noticing it or singling it out for attack.

Nowadays, after the placenta is delivered and the cord cut, the women wipe some of the excess blood and vernix off with leaves or a cloth, make sure the child is breathing, and then lay it on a net bag, cloth, or leaves to dry off. It is believed that should the baby stay wet, it may become sickly and die.

There is considerable variation in bathing practices for newborns. Many are never bathed; others, particularly those whose mothers have had more outside contact, are bathed almost daily beginning a few days after birth. Newborns are usually bathed in the village rather than in the cold river. Some mothers heat water in cans, dipping it out with their hands to wash the child's body.

Not long after birth, one of the women present holds the baby in her lap and, applying slight pressure, gently kneads the head with an upward motion. The purpose of this action is to hasten the bones growing together at the fontanel.

Feeding. An infant is not nursed by its mother until her breast milk comes in. The colustrum is considered unhealthy for the child, so in the interim period one or more other women may nurse the child. Thereafter, nursing is on demand and is used as one of the primary ways of comforting a crying child. If a mother becomes pregnant, she stops nursing her youngest child. It is rare for a child not to be weaned before the next is born. In the past, sexual relations were not resumed until the child was able to chew and swallow food on its own.

The first taste of solid food that a baby had in the past and is sometimes given today is taro (*am*). Long ago when Doyap first created the world, it is said that a woman had a crying child who could not be comforted. She tried giving it breast milk, but it refused it and kept on crying. So she took a bit of taro, chewed it up, and gave it to the child. This food succeeded in quieting the child and Ketengban mothers have carried on this practice.

There is a second and perhaps more substantial reason in the eyes of the Ketengban for giving taro to newborns. The spirits, it seems, are always on the lookout for people who have become sick and have stopped eating. In this weakened condition their hearts or souls are considered "ripe" for the spirits to eat. If a newborn is only getting breast milk and the spirits do not see any residue of taro inside the lower end of the child's intestines, they regard the baby to be the same as sick people who are not eating at all and come to "eat" the child. Therefore, the mother puts some taro into the mouth of the child so that the taste or essence will go into the end of the intestine to be seen by the spirits. Seeing this substance the spirits think, "They want to keep this child. This one is not for me to have," and thus leave the child alone. Again, this practice has its roots in the mythology as described earlier.

Fretfulness and Crying. The cause of fretful, crying babies was often traditionally associated with harrassment by spirits. One of these spirits was *kinodapdapkor ner,* a female spirit in the form of a type of owl, described as having a wide "frog mouth." She would come to the house flapping her wings to startle the baby, causing it to cry. Crying until its throat became dry, the child would eventually choke and die. To combat this possible eventuality, the mother would take a piece of *ba co* wood,[4] and wave it around in the direction of the ceiling. Then she would throw it up to punch a hole in the roof and fly out. As she was doing this, she would repeat the spell, "I am breaking your wings. I am making you weak." By performing this action she was rendering the spirit useless and thereby ending the harrassment. By forcibly propelling the stick out of the house, she was by associative magic expelling the invisible owl, i.e., in essence, exorcising the spirit from the house.

Another cause for excessive crying could be remedied by offering pork to the offending spirit. The cheek of a freshly killed pig was placed in the house on the edge of the small wood-drying platform over the fire facing the door. In this way the spirit could see the pork from the front door and be enticed into eating it instead of bothering the baby. The cheek of the pig is important because this is the spot on which Um Bo was thought to have marked his own pigs with red clay as a sign of ownership. The sacrifice of the pig jowl venerates him, recalls his presence, and entreats his power to expel the threatening female spirit, who is ultimately under his authority.

---

[4]*ba co* is the type of wood that Um Bo was tied to when he was killed. For a discussion of this belief, see the article by Andrew Sims in this volume.

Care of the Mother

During the time that the woman stayed in the birthing house, she subsisted on food that she or her husband had brought there prior to her entering it. He could also bring food, firewood, and more leaves for her to sit on after the delivery. Standing at a distance from the house, he would lay the items down, call to her, and then leave. When he was gone, his wife could come and retrieve the things. An attending woman, if there was one, could also provide what was needed.

Today, as in the past, the attending women assist in caring for the postpartum woman for the first several days until she is able to get around by herself. They dispose of the leaves she has been sitting on and the ones the baby has defecated on and keep her supplied with fresh ones. They also bring her water, food, and firewood. This is, in fact, what happens in most cases. However, if she happens to have no relatives (or very few) living in her village, she may get little assistance of this kind. Her husband may bring her some of these things, but the food is usually meager since men are not the gardeners.

Foods. There are several foods that are considered good to eat after giving birth, mostly those that are felt to be soft and tasty and easy on the stomach. Some of them are traditionally eaten by women at this time, although in questioning women about it, they do not feel any compulsion to continue this tradition. A few of these foods are *gwei am* (see *gwei am* in the section on Reincorporation below) and *tolopa*, two types of jungle greens, and *tepmeng*, a type of wild raspberry. Whereas two types of sugarcane were eaten in the past to aid in bringing in the mother's milk supply, papaya is now the preferred food. In addition to these initial foods, other staple foods that appeal to her at the time are eaten, such as sweet potatoes, bananas, and manioc. In the Ketengban woman's opinion, it is important for her to eat in order to fill up the now empty space where the baby was. In actual fact, from what I have observed, women eat nearly anything that is brought if it tastes good to them. Some women are well-cared for and others have very little to eat. This is a reflection, in part, of how good a network of kinsmen and mutual obligations the woman has established.

Drinking Water Ritual. As mentioned earlier, in times past there was an obligatory abstinence from water for the first few days after the birth. This ritual is called *me tu tandyena*. Mothers who had given birth to a male child got their first taste of water on the third day and those who gave birth to a female child on the fourth day. The difference was attributed to the fact that the spirits of males were stronger than those of females and could therefore handle water sooner. This first drink was given by a man from a specific type of gourd, called *buk mau*. One is reminded of Ketengban mythology which purports that from the beginning all the waters were stored by Doyap in a *buk mau* gourd at Limgonai mountain, the center of creation. Rain was thought to be the result of this gourd being tipped over on the different mountain tops. Small streams and rivers were from small holes or the overflow from the gourd. As the man gave the water to the mother, he repeated within the woman's hearing, *mukupe, doponge, kwakone*, which means, 'I am diverting the waters of the Mukupe and the Doponge Rivers'. These two rivers are the main ones flowing off the mountain top where one of the main ceremonial houses was built. This was only said for the benefit of the woman hearing it. The actual spell was said under the man's breath or in his mind. For the woman to hear these taboo words would have resulted in great calamity.

Reincorporation

Traditionally, on the day following the breaking of the water fast, the mother returned with her child to her house in the village. Before she came, the ritual specialists performed a ritual near the door of the house. The scent gland of a cuscus was rubbed on a rock, which in turn was placed upside down on the ground on top of the scent gland in front of the doorway to the house. This was done as a diversionary measure against the female spirits (*ketlingna ner* and *yami ner*) who might try to steal the spirit of the child. Thus, if the spirit approached the house and caught the scent of the cuscus, she would think it had been killed for her, eat that, and leave the child alone. The significance of the rock being turned over was to shut the door (*bublan dengdongona*) of the rotten, hollow trees through which these kinds of spirits characteristically entered the world of men. These hollow trees formed a sort of underground tunnel transit system through which powerful spirits traveled about the land. A certain type of tree nut was also placed under this rock in hopes of preventing the child from experiencing an early death; for just as the tree nut falls quickly to the ground, the child could die before reaching old age. Two pieces of *ba co* were also important in the ritual. One was placed alongside the climbing pole leading from the ground to the house and remained there for some time afterwards. The second piece was stuck in the ground on top of the rock with the scent gland and nut under it. This one could be taken out soon. As the woman entered the house, she had to touch or grasp the piece stuck in the ground and step on the other placed alongside the pole ladder lest the precautions taken earlier would fail to be effective.

In addition, if the child was a male, a type of taro (*kwa am yal*) was planted nearby. This particular species always produces at least two tubers, which branch into two joined tubers instead of a single root. It was thought that to plant this type of taro would ensure many more male children being born to the mother. If the child was a female, a *gwei am* was planted. The *gwei am* resembles a taro plant but produces no tubers so it symbolizes the hope that no more female children would be born. It is said to have grown plentifully in Daibalal, the river area where the cultural hero, Um Bo, told women to dwell. Thus, the leaves of it have long been considered a staple for women. The female spirit (*daiyankar ner*) originating from this place, also had a great liking for this plant. By planting it near the house of a newborn female child, it was thought that she would eat the plant leaves instead of "eating" or taking away the spirit of the baby.

Leaf Bundle Ritual

From the time of a baby's birth until about six months of age, precautions were taken to ward off attacks by three specific types of spirits. This was effected by the use of leaf bundles called *me pona*. These bundles could be prepared by either men or women but were more commonly made by the woman's husband, by her birthing assistant, or even later by the woman herself. If the husband prepared the bundles for her before she left the birthing house, he would either give them to another woman to give to his wife or he would stand at a distance from the house, toss them near the door, call to his wife, and then leave. This distance was maintained to avoid any possible contact with blood or secretions from the birthing process.

The bundles consisted of any of the following types of leaves, all of which were considered to have a strong, pleasant smell: *kelkel bo, golum bo, kulamdaro bo, nor bo,* and *warup bo*. The main function of the leaves was to camouflage the baby's scent with their own smell, thus preventing the spirits from picking up and following the child's trail in order to steal its soul or "eat" it. These bundles were placed on mountain tops, river banks, densely wooded areas, and any other places that spirits were known to inhabit. This ritual was a daily occurrence that was repeated any time the mother ventured outside of the immediate village area. After putting the bundle on the ground, she would step on it first before proceeding down the trail or crossing the river. Before crossing a river, bundles were placed on the riverbank because it was believed that spirits in the form of frogs, tadpoles, bugs, and eels would follow the scent of any fluids from the birth (*mi kawa*) which might fall in the river and thus cause the child's death. The smell from the leaves would drive these spirits away and prevent such harm to the child.

The three types of jungle-dwelling spirits who are thought to steal a child's soul are: *gup-gup ngop*, those who pick up a person's scent and follow him or her; *epu ngebo*, those who see the person; and *co yapne ning*, those who do not directly cause the baby to become suddenly ill and die, but prevent it from thriving and, therefore, it eventually dies while still an infant.

Return to Daily Routine

Finally, the mother goes to the river to bathe after the heaviest bleeding has slowed and she feels strong enough to get around. Bathing usually takes place around the second day but may not be until a week or more after the birth. She usually resumes her daily routine of gardening and caring for the pigs by the fourth or fifth day after giving birth, taking her newborn with her in a net bag wherever she goes.

Conclusion

I have attempted to show how Ketengban pregnancy and childbirth practices are rooted in their mythology and reflect their world view. The Ketengban world view has, in some ways, been changing in the last decade and a half, as they have come into more contact with the outside world. As a natural result, many of the practices concerning pregnancy and childbirth have also changed. I have in this paper, however, attempted to report both traditional practices as well as current practices.

References

Faithhorn, Elizabeth. 1976. Aspects of female life and male-female relations among the Kafe. In Paula Brown and Georgeda Buchbinder (eds.), Man and woman in the New Guinea Highlands. Washington, D.C.: American Anthropological Association 8:87.

Heeschen, Volker. 1978. The Mek languages of Irian Jaya, with special reference to the Eipo language. Irian 7(2):3–46. Abepura: Cenderawasih University.

Ryan, Peter, ed. 1972. Religion and magic. Encyclopaedia of Papua and New Guinea 2:1003. Melbourne: Melbourne University Press.

Schiefenhovel, Von G. und W. Eipo. n.d. Irian Jaya: Vorgange bei der Geburt eines Mädchens und Anderung der Infantizid-Absicht. Human-ethnologisches Filmarchiv: Humanethologisches Filmarchiv der Max-Planck-Gesellschaft.

Sims, Andrew. 1986. Ketengban kinship. Irian 14:15–44. Abepura: Cenderawasih University.

———. 1992. Ketengban rituals. In Joyce Sterner and Marilyn Gregerson (eds.), Rituals and relationships in the Valley of the Sun: The Ketengban of Irian Jaya. This volume.

The Clans That Birthed Me: Ketengban Kinship

Andrew Sims with Joyce Sterner

Contents

The Clans That Birthed Me: Ketengban Kinship

For the Ketengban, kinship involves not only terms and the associated genealogical relationships but complex sets of role expectations and interpersonal behavioral obligations for each particular relationship. A study of kinship terminology confirms the Ketengban emphasis on male dominance revealed in their cosmology (see Andrew Sims, this volume).[1] The most basic kin terms in ego's and descending generations refer to males unless marked by the adjective *ner* 'female'; thus the unmarked terms have a male referent. The system features the ideal of marriage to mother's brother's daughter, either real or classificatory, and would traditionally be called patrilineal. There is, however, an unusual emphasis on bilateral bloodlines, which dictates that any woman of any age of both grandmothers' clans is called grandmother because "she is of the clan that birthed my parents." The importance of bloodlines can easily be seen in that many affines in the first and second ascending generations are

---

[1]Data for this paper were gathered by Andrew Sims during periods of living in the village of Omban between February 1981 and September 1983. The original version of the paper was written during a six-week workshop held in October and November 1983, conducted by the Summer Institute of Linguistics working in cooperation with Cenderawasih University. Elias Basinye, Pius Kulka, and Amos Kulka, all Ketengban speakers from Omban, along with many of their friends and kinsmen, helped in gathering and refining the material. During the actual drafting of the paper, Wayne Dye gave helpful comments and Lloyd Peckham gave invaluable advice and suggestions. A major revision of this paper took place in early 1991 and involved extending the data to the second degree of collaterality, preparing charts of terms, and noting the themes present in Ketengban kinship.

known as "the spouse of my —" if there is no consanguineal relationship. Additionally, bloodlines are emphasized in mother's clan not only by the typical Melanesian importance of mother's brother, but also in that mother's brother's children and their patrilateral descendants are called by the same cross-cousin (*neiki*) kin terms. They also call ego 'child' regardless of respective age. The terms for male child and female child in the first descending generation extend to all succeeding descending generations, so there is no specific terminology for grandchildren or great-grandchildren. This lack of distinctives in descending generations is additional evidence of the emphasis placed on ego's own heritage and bloodlines.

A further constraint on Ketengban kin term usage is the emphasis on maintaining good relationships and making other people feel good. This emphasis influences kin terms greatly: if alter is even slightly older than ego, or if the normal kin term for alter does not indicate the true closeness of the relationship, then a closer kin term (or one from an ascending generation) will be used for alter. Thus, if an affine (e.g., mother's brother's wife) is likely to be offended by the use of a nonconsanguineal term, the Ketengban will courteously use a consanguineal or friendship term to make her feel better.

This paper is divided into three major sections: a description of kinship terminology, a delineation of the mutual rights and obligations of the most important Ketengban relationships as a key to understanding Ketengban social structure, and a discussion of some of the mental strategies used by the Ketengban both for determining what relationship a particular individual may have with them and for teaching the system to children.

Kinship Terminology

Ketengban kinship terminology is characterized by bifurcate merging terminology in the first ascending generation while merging the terms used for grandmother and father's sister (*nau*)[2]. In ego's generation, the terminology classifies parallel cousins with siblings while normally distinguishing matrilateral

---

[2]Spelling of Ketengban words in this paper follows the analysis done by Sims (1981) and follows usage in the Central dialect. All kin terms are inalienably possessed, i.e., are used in conjunction with personal pronouns. In the case of some terms like -*apke*, the morphological processes involved render a term *napke* for the first person, but *er apke* would be appropriate for third person. The term *nau* remains the same throughout, *ne nau*, *er nau*, but not *er au* 'my grandmother, his grandmother'; *ne nai*,

cross-cousins from patrilateral cross-cousins and from parallel kinsmen. Patrilateral cross-cousins are usually called by the same terminology as one's children, but may be referred to reciprocally by the matrilateral cross-cousin term, if desired. Relative age is only marked among parallel cousins and siblings.

All singular kin terms distinguish the sex of alter (see figure 1). The basic kin terms for affines and for consanguineal kin in ego's generation and descending generations designate a male unless the female term *ner* is added. There is also a male term *bo* which is optionally used. This usage is consonant with the male dominance theme throughout Ketengban culture. There are three terms used exclusively by male ego (*nernye* 'brother-in-law', *ne ner* 'my woman [wife]', *mal ner* 'sister') and two others used exclusively by female ego (*ninge* 'husband', *malnye* 'brother').

English Gloss	Ketengban Singular	Ketengban Plural
ancestors	*deirin ngop, co deiyo ngop, co puna ngop*	*co deiyo nerape, co deiyo neng, co puna neng*
grandfather	*apke, apu bo*	*apu yape*
grandmother	*nau*	*nau yapu*
father	*nai, atok*	*nai yape, natok yapu*
mother	*nin, nanin, nainkon, ne nong ner*	*nanin yape, nainkon yape, ne nong nerepe*
maternal uncle	*mam*	*mam yape*
child	*mi, ner mi*	*nyape*
sisters (m. sp.)	*mal ner*	*mal nerepe, mal nerapu*
brothers (f. sp.)	*malnye*	*mal nenge*
older sibling	*tat, du, tat ner, du ner*	*tat yape, du yape, tat nerepe, du nerepe*
younger sibling	*weit, weit ner*	*weit yape, weit nerepe*
cross-cousin	*neiki (bo), neiki ner*	*neiki yape, neiki nerepe*
brother-in-law (m. sp.)	*nernye*	*ner neng*
parent, child-in-law	*yamal (bo), yamal ner*	*yamal yapu, yamal nerapu*

Fig. 1. Ketengban singular and plural kin terms

---

er nai, not *er ai* 'my father, his father'. There is some difference between person categories in the terms used. Thus ego would, in reference to mother, say *nainkon* or *nanin* 'my mother', but in referring to the mother of a third party one would say *er nin*, not *er ainkon*. Therefore, the terms used in this paper are those used by ego in reference to his own kinsmen where ego is a single individual (first person singular).

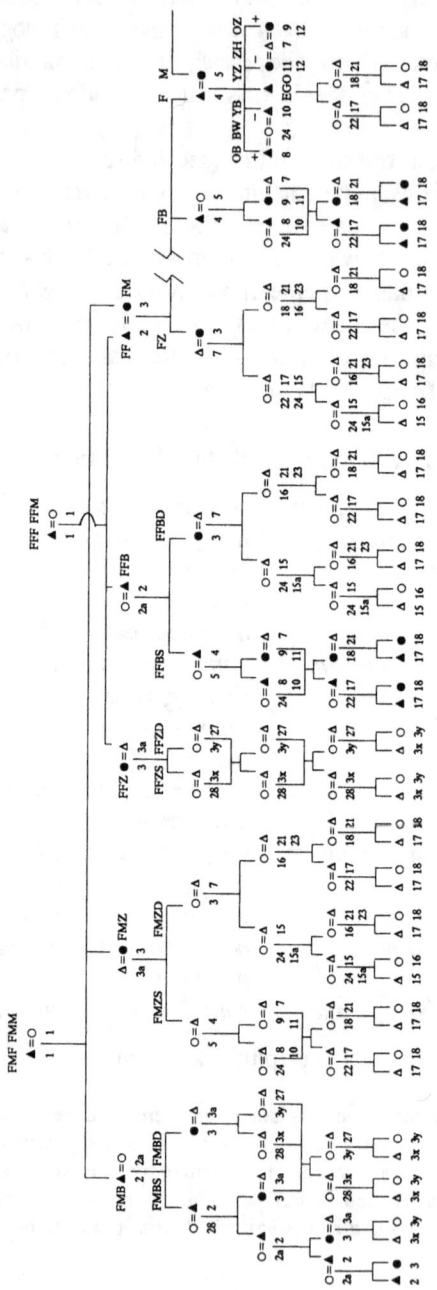

If any of the male or female affines on this chart are from either of ego's grandmother's clans they will be called nau 'grandmother'.

A number followed by a means that that person is called the spouse of the person indicated, e.g. 6a mam ner 'mother's brother's wife'. A number followed by x means the son of the indicated relative; when followed by y it means the daughter of the indicated relative, e.g., 3x 'grandmother's son' and 3y 'grandmother's daughter'. Two numbers under the same name indicate alternate nomenclature.

Those terms differing for female egos from those on this chart are: #8 and #10 could additionally be called #13; all #7 would become #23.

Because the terms used by women only are so few and they are described in the text, a separate chart for female ego is not included.

(continued)

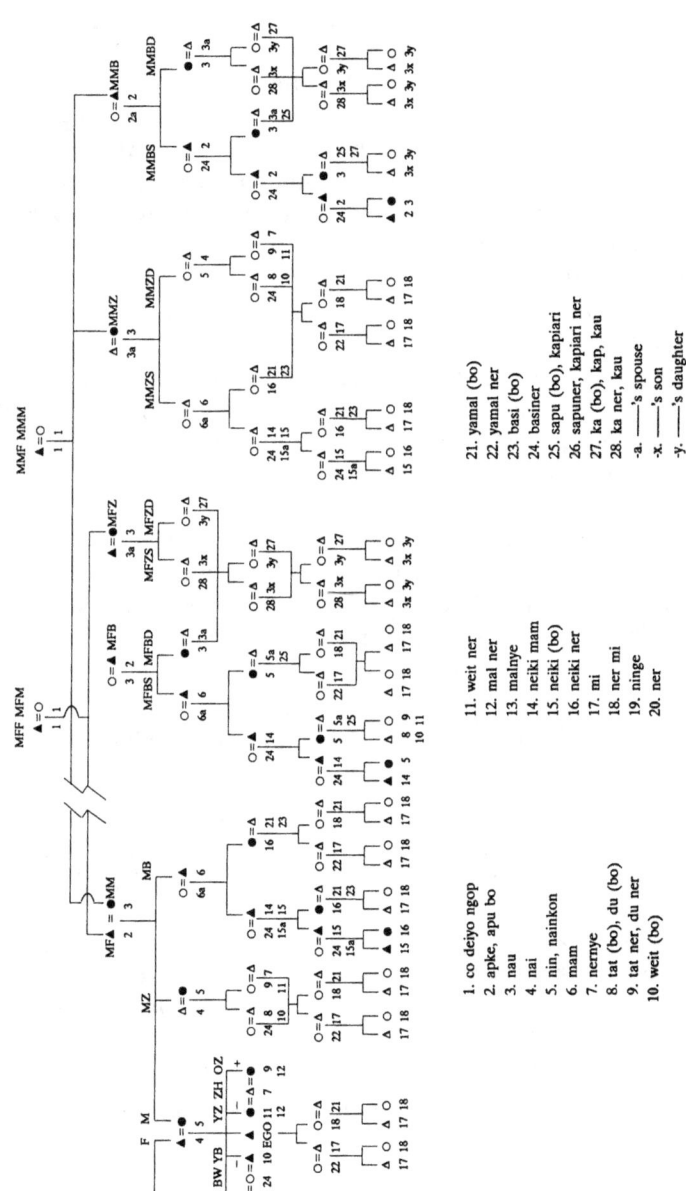

1. co deiyo ngop
2. apke, apu bo
3. nau
4. nai
5. nin, nainkon
6. mam
7. nemye
8. tat (bo), du (bo)
9. tat ner, du ner
10. weit (bo)

11. weit ner
12. mal ner
13. malnye
14. neiki mam
15. neiki (bo)
16. neiki ner
17. mi
18. ner mi
19. ninge
20. ner

21. yamal (bo)
22. yamal ner
23. basi (bo)
24. basiner
25. sapu (bo), kapiari
26. sapuner, kapiari ner
27. ka (bo), kap, kau
28. ka ner, kau
-a. ——'s spouse
-x. ——'s son
-y. ——'s daughter

Fig. 2. Ketengban consanguineal kinship chart

Consanguineal Kinship Terms

Ketengban consanguineal kinship terms are presented in figure 2. These terms, although constant in theory, are subject to the constraints of age and respect mentioned above and are described in detail in the final section on mental strategies. The terms for affines included on the consanguineal chart are additionally subject to the constraint that any man or woman of either grandmother's clan is called *apke* 'grandfather' or *nau* 'grandmother' regardless of their age or other relationship to ego. The term *mam* 'mother's brother' is used by ego to refer to any man whom his mother calls brother (*malnye*) regardless of other clan affiliation to ego. Since the Ketengban cultural ideal is to marry mother's brother's real or classificatory daughter, these constraints dictate much of the average Ketengban person's kinship terminology. For example, if mother's brother's wife is of grandmother's clan, as she would be if mother's brother married his own mother's brother's daughter, she is called *nau* 'grandmother'; if not, she is called *mam ner* 'mother's brother's woman'. However, father's sister is *always* called *nau* 'grandmother'. Figure 2 gives the terms as unaffected by these constraints.

There are some differences between terms of reference and terms of address, the primary one being that a diminutive suffix -*o* may be added to any kin term for use in addressing alter. Figure 3 shows the Ketengban kin terms which have different address forms including the diminutive form.

English Gloss	Reference Term	Address Term
grandfather	*apu (bo), apke*	*apuo, apko*
grandmother	*nau*	*nauo*
father	*nai, natok*	*nai, naio*, natoko*
mother	*nin, nainkon*	*nanin(o), nainkon(o)*
mother's brother	*mam*	*mam(o)*
male cross-cousin	*neiki bo, neiki*	*mio, neiko, neiki bo*
female cross-cousin	*neiki ner*	*ner mi, na neiki nero*
child	*mi, ner mi*	*amio, naio*, anero*
wife	*ner*	*ka nero, anero, ne ner*
husband	*ninge*	*kao, ning(o)*

*Father and child of either sex may use this reciprocal diminutive address form.

Fig. 3. Ketengban terms of reference and address

Grandkinsmen. In the second ascending generation, two basic terms are used: one for male grandkinsmen, *apke* 'grandfather', and one for female grandkinsmen, *nau* 'grandmother'. These terms extend to collateral consanguineal kinsmen of that generation, but the only affine in this generation to be called this term is mother's father's brother's wife. All other affines are called by the descriptive phrase "——'s spouse." Only sex is distinguished by these terms, not bifurcation or relative age. Thus father's father's brother and mother's mother's brother are referred to as *apke*, and father's father's sister and mother's mother's sister are referred to as *nau*. (The plural forms, address forms, and alternate forms of these terms are listed in figures 1 and 3 and appendix 2 respectively.)[3] The additional distinctive use of these two terms for all males and females of any age of either grandmother's clan is easily seen in figure 2.

Grandchildren and great-grandchildren are referred to by the same terms as children, described below. This lack of emphasis on succeeding generations reemphasizes the paramount importance of the bloodlines which "have birthed" ego.

Parent-child. To designate kinsmen of the parent and child generations $(+1, -1)$, the Ketengban employ five terms. Of these, four terms classify consanguineal kinsmen of the first ascending generation above ego within the first degree of collaterality. They are *nai* 'father', *nainkon* 'mother', *mam* 'mother's brother', and *nau* 'father's sister (grandmother)'.

These terms distinguish both sex and bifurcation, two referring to parallel kinsmen and two to cross-kinsmen. Parallel and cross are defined as in Seneca (Lounsbury 1964), by the sex of kinsmen of the first ascending generation above ego. Within the genealogical chain that links ego to alter, if the sex of the two kinsmen of the first ascending generation is the same, they are parallel kinsmen; if their sex is different they are cross-kinsmen. The sex of linking kinsmen of other generations is irrelevant. Thus, all men of mother's generation whom she calls brother are *mam* 'maternal uncle'

---

[3]Many of the terms have alternates which are in quite common usage. Sometimes there is a difference in nuance of meaning or a slight emphasis on one component over another. In other cases there is no discernible difference. Similarly, there are a few dialectical differences in some terms where one area may prefer one choice over another or even exclusively use one term. However, all the terms seem to be common knowledge throughout the area. This paper follows usage in the Central dialect and Omban village. I make no effort to include all the dialectical variants, but a list of some common alternates for terms in the Central dialect and their meanings (if notable) can be found in appendix 2.

as is mother's mother's sister's son. All men of mother's maternal clan are called *apke* 'grandfather' no matter what their age relative to ego. All men of father's generation and clan are *nai* 'father', as is father's mother's sister's son and mother's sister's husband, and their spouses are always *nin* or *nainkon* 'mother'. As previously stated, matrilateral cross-cousin marriage is the preferred form, so father's sister may in fact be mother's brother's wife, i.e., a man of ego's mother's clan and generation, whom ego designates as *mam* 'mother's brother', is likely to be married to a woman of ego's clan whom ego designates as *nau* 'grandmother'.

In cases in which one wishes to distinguish one's biological parent from their siblings or clan members, the term *sisa* 'true' or 'real' is added. This term may, in turn, be said of maternal uncles and paternal aunts to distinguish them from others in their clan. In the case of mother, one could alternately say *nainkon sisa* 'real mother' or *nenong nerepe* 'my body woman' (she who brought me into being). Similarly, the term *gwanamne* 'to adopt and care for' is added to designate foster or stepparent, or *gwanamna mi* 'adopted child'. The parent terms also apply to spouses of parallel kinsmen of the parent generation as stated above.

The terms *mi* 'male child' and *ner mi* 'female child' are the reciprocal of *nai* 'father', *nainkon* 'mother', *mam* 'mother's brother,' and *nau* 'grandmother (paternal aunt)' in the parental generation and of the grandparent terms as well. They may also be the reciprocal of *neiki mam sisa* 'true mother's brother's son' and *neiki ner sisa* 'true mother's brother's daughter' regardless of the relative ages of ego and alter. For example, mother's brother's children call ego *mi* 'male child'. Reciprocally, ego may call father's sister's children (+1) 'child'. Some Ketengban say that these terms extend down to all generations and conversely up to father's father's sister's children's children. However, other Ketengban disagree. It would appear that the sociological significance of such a remote relationship does not demand consistent designation. The kinship chart in figure 2 which is based on Ketengban usage of kinship terms does, in some respects, reflect this inconsistency.

The terms for child do not extend to the spouses of children but may be extended when used by ego in conjunction with the first person plural pronoun *nun* 'our', as in *nun mi* 'our (male) children', to refer to all male kinsmen of the second descending generation (−2) without bifurcate distinctions. In the singular forms, however, the bifurcate distinctions must be maintained as in the first descending generation. Children of both sexes may be referred to collectively by the plural term *nyape* (see figure 1).

Siblings. In ego's generation, priority of parallel kin is based on age relative to ego whether or not alter is an actual biological sibling. Two terms are used for older siblings, *du* or *tat* 'older male sibling' and *du ner* and *tat ner* 'older female sibling'. There is one term for younger siblings, *weit* 'younger male sibling' and *weit ner* 'younger female sibling'. Male sex is also optionally designated by adding the word *bo* 'man' or 'male' to the base forms *du, tat,* or *weit*. For example, ego may refer to his older male sibling as *du* or *du bo* 'older male sibling' and his older female sibling as *du ner* 'older female sibling, but not simply as *du*. Ego may also optionally refer to siblings of the opposite sex without distinguishing relative age. A male ego designates his sister as *mal ner* and his sisters collectively as *mal nerepe,* or *nerapu*. A female ego designates her brother as *malnye* and her brothers collectively as *mal nenge*. These terms extend collaterally to any opposite sex parallel kinsmen of ego's generation. Similarly, one's siblings may be referred to collectively as *weitapselip* 'sibling' or *weitedu* 'younger-older ones'. These terms of reference may be used by either male or female ego and do not distinguish gender.

Among cross-kinsmen, no distinction is made as to age relative to ego or age relative to other cross-kinsmen within a generation. Gender, however, is always marked in the singular forms. Ego's male matrilateral cross-cousin is called *neiki mam* or *neiki bo* 'male cross-cousin' and his female cross-cousin is referred to as *neiki ner* 'female cross-cousin' while the general plural form is *neiki yape* 'cross cousins'. They in turn usually refer to ego as *ne mi* 'my (male) child' or *ne ner mi* 'my female child'. These terms are sometimes said to extend to all patrilineal descendants of mother's brother and reciprocally back to ego. Children of *neiki ner* 'female cross cousin' are called *mi* 'son' and *ner mi* 'daughter'. Father's sister's children are usually referred to as son and daughter, but may optionally be called *neiki bo* or *neiki ner,* probably because ego is their *neiki mam* 'mother's brother's child', a strong bond in Ketengban culture.

A slightly simpler and different way of looking at Ketengban kinship terms is to define what ego will call the children or spouses of certain relatives. The children of those whom ego calls 'mother' and 'father' are always siblings to ego, and their children are always called ego's children. The children of those called 'mother's brother' are called *neiki* 'cross-cousin'. However, the children of all male cross-cousins continue to be called *neiki* through all descending generations, while ego calls children of any female cross-cousin 'child'.

In ascending generations the only consistency found in terms used for spouses is that of those called mother and father. That is, a woman called mother is always married to a man called father. This does not hold true in ego's generation or lower. However, women ego called *nau* 'grand-mother' or 'paternal aunt' can be married to men called by a number of different terms. Men whom ego called 'grandfather' may be married to women ego called 'grandfather's wife', *ka ner* 'friend (female)' or *basi ner* 'sister-in-law' depending on their exact relationship to ego.

The children of a woman called *nau* 'grandmother' (or 'paternal aunt') who is not of ego's clan or his mother's nuclear family are usually called *nau mi* 'grandmother's son' or *nau ner mi* 'grandmother's daughter'. Some-times they are alternatively called *ka bo* 'male friend' or *ka ner* 'female friend' as are their children. This again is further evidence of the heavy emphasis the Ketengban place on "the clans that birthed me."

It may be noted also, in studying figure 2, that terms for various consanguineal kin are not confined to their primary generational slots. Thus, what ego calls any individual depends on what he calls his parents, taking into account their clan membership. It cannot be overemphasized that both maternal and paternal clan connections are an overriding con-straint on what a kinsman is called. See figures 6 to 10 (pages 146ff) as additional illustrations of this.

Affinal Kinship Terms

Ketengban affinal kinship terms are presented in figures 4 and 5. These terms distinguish sex of alter and are again subject to the constraint mentioned earlier that if any of the men or women belong to either of ego's grandmother's clans they are called *apke* 'grandfather' or *nau* 'grand-mother' rather than any other kin term.

Familial Affinal Terms. The term *yamal* 'parent-in-law, child-in-law $(+2, +1, -1, -2)$' is another term which used by itself signifies males and which takes the added optional male term *bo* and female term *ner*. The terms *yamal bo* 'father-in-law, son-in-law' and *yamal ner* 'mother-in-law, daughter-in-law' designate all of spouse's bilateral kinsmen and their spouses of the parent and ascending generations. Accordingly, husband's father and wife's father are both *yamal bo* 'father-in-law' and husband's mother and wife's mother are *yamal ner* 'mother-in-law'. Therefore, either a man or a woman refers to his or her spouse's parents or grandparents

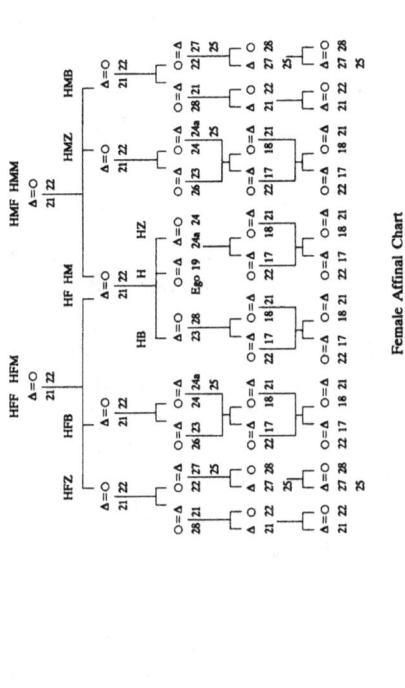

Male Affinal Chart

Female Affinal Chart

*If any affine is consanguineally related to ego, then the closest appropriate term is used.

7. nernye	17. mi	23. basi (bo)
8. tat (bo), du (bo)	18. ner mi	24. basi ner
9. tat ner, du ner	19. ninge	25. sapu (bo), kaplari
10. weit (bo)	20. ner	26. sapu ner, kaplari ner
11. weit ner	21. yamal (bo)	27. ka (bo), kap, kau
	22. yamal ner	28. ka ner, kau
		-a. ——'s spouse

Fig. 4. Ketengban affinal kinship chart

of either sex by the basic term *yamal* plus the sex distinguishing adjective. This term further extends to collateral kinsmen of affines in the first and additional ascending generations. In descending generations it is used for 'son's wife', 'daughter's husband' and the spouses of all ego's classificatory children.

Siblings-in-law. There are three terms which denote affinal kinsmen of the same generation as ego or his spouse and extend to all kinsmen. The basic term *basi* is male unless distinguished by the usual male/female adjectives. It is used whenever either one or both of ego and alter is female. The term *nernye* 'brother-in-law' is used only between two males.

The term *basi ner* 'sister-in-law' is a term used by a male or female ego to denote any female affine, i.e., any woman a spouse or sibling's spouse refers to by one of the female sibling terms (*weit ner, du ner*). Ego's brother's spouse is also referred to by this term. On the consanguineal chart, the wife of *neiki mam* or *neiki bo* 'cross-cousin' may be called *basi ner* or alternatively she may be called 'my cross-cousin's wife'. The spouse of a male of mother's mother's clan called 'grandfather' is also called *basi ner*.

As stated above, *nernye* 'man's brother-in-law' is a reciprocal term used by a male ego to a male affine, e.g., sister's husband, wife's brother and their classificatory extensions. Female ego uses the term *basi bo* '(woman's) brother-in-law' to refer to any man her brother calls *neryne* and also any kinsman a husband or sister's husband refers to by one of the male sibling terms. Female ego's sister's husband is also referred to by this term. The men whom she refers to as *basi bo* reciprocate by referring to her as *basi ner* 'sister-in-law'.

Some Ketengban say that, rather than using the term *basi bo* for husband's sister's husband, it is correct for female ego to refer to him with the descriptive phrase *ne basi ner er ninge* 'the husband of my sister-in-law'. Again, if there are actual clan or closer consanguineal connections to alter, these terms would normally supersede the use of the affinal terms.

Spouses. The basic terms of reference for spouses are *ninge* 'husband' and *ner* 'woman'. These are normally preceded by the modifier *ne* 'my'. If, in accordance with levirate marriage patterns, a man takes his deceased brother's wife, he may refer to her as his *soli ner* or *soli daksi ner* 'widow wife' or 'the widow wife I picked'. If a man has more than one wife, but the additional wives are not levirate wives, he may refer to them as his *tarumne ner* 'additional wives'. A man may refer to these or any of his wives simply as *ner* 'wife', or again in the case of multiple wives he may refer to the first as *men ner* 'first wife' and later wives as *tarumne* or *amenda ner* 'later wife'. Women who are co-wives of the same man may, to express friendship and equality or to be informal, refer to each other as *ka ner* 'female friend'. Other options are for the first wife, whether she is older or not, to refer to the second wife as *ner mi* 'female child'; and the second wife to the first as *nainkon* 'mother'. Where relations are good, should the second wife be older than the first, the first would respectfully refer to the older as *nainkon* and this could be reciprocated by *ner mi* 'my child' by the older to younger, or they might refer to one another as *nainkon* 'mother'. The quality of the women's mutual relationship is a key determining factor here. If there are genealogical connections between the two women or their clans, the appropriate term based on this relationship would be used. Figure 5 below lists affinal kinship terms.

Term	Nearest Designation	Consanguineal	Affinal
1. *co deiyo ngop* *co puna ngop*	great-grandparent	PPP	
2. *apke*	grandfather	FF, MF, FFB, MFB, FMB MMB, FMBS, MMBS, FMBSS MMBSS, FMBSSS, MMBSSS FMBSSSS, MMBSSSS	
3. *nau*	grandmother	FM, MM, FFZ, FMZ MFZ, MMZ, FMBD, FMZD MFBD, MMBD, FMBSD MMBSD, FMBSSD, MMBSSD FMBSSSD, MMBSSSD	MFBW
	father's sister	FZ, FFBD	
4. *nai*	father	F, FB, FFBS, FMZS	MZH, MMZDH
5. *nainkon* *nin, nanin*	mother	M, MZ, MMZD, MFBSD MFBSSD, MFBSSSD	FBW, FFBSW FMZSW
6. *mam*	maternal uncle	MB, MFBS, MMZS	
7. *nemye*	brother-in-law (male ego)		ZH, FZH, FBDH, MZDH FFBDH, FMZDH FFBSDH, FMZSDH MMZDDH, MFBSDCDH WB, WFBS, WMZS
8. *du (bo)* *tat (bo)*	older brother (if older than ego)	OB FBS, MZS, FFBSS, FMZSS MMZDS, MFBSSDS	
9. *du ner* *tat ner*	older sister (if older than ego)	OZ FBD, MZD, FFBSD, FMZSD MMZDD, MFBSSDD	
10. *weit (bo)*	younger brother (if younger than ego)	YB FBS, MZS, FFBSS, FMZSS MMZDS, MFBSSDS	

(continued)

Andrew Sims with Joyce Sterner

Term	Nearest Designation	Consanguineal	Affinal
11. *weit ner*	younger sister (if younger than ego)	YZ FBD, MZD, FFBSD, FMZSD MMZDD, MFBSSDD	
12. *mal ner*	sister (male ego)	Z	
13. *malnye*	brother (female ego)	B (not on chart)	
14. *neiki mam*	matrilateral male cross-cousin	MBS, MFBSS, MMZSS MFBSSS, MFBSSSS	
15. *neiki (bo)*	male cross-cousin	FZS, MBS, FZSS, MBSS FFBDS, FMZDS, MMZSS FZSSS, MBSSS, MMZSSS FFBDSS, FMZDSS FFBDSSS, FMZDSSS MMZSSSS	
16. *neiki ner*	female cross-cousin	FZD, MBD, FZSD, MBSD FZSSD, MBSSD, MMZSD FFBDD, FMZDD, FFBDSD FMZDSD, MMZSSD FFBDSSD, FMZDSSD MMZSSSD	
17. *mi*	son	S, BS, ZS, CS, BCS, ZCS FZS, FBCS, FZDS, MBDS MZCS, FBCCS, FZSDS FZDCS, MBSDS, MBDCS MZCCS, FFBSCS, FFBDDS FMZSCS, FMZDDS MFBSDS, MMZSDS MMZDCS, FFBDSDS FFBDDCS, FFBSCCS FMZSCCS, FMZDSDS FMZDDCS, MFBSDCS MMZSSDS, MMZSDCS MMZDCCS	HBS, WBS, HZS, WZS HBCS, WBCS HZCS, WZCS HFBCS, WFBCS HMZCS, WMZCS HFBCCS, WFBCCS HMZCCS, WMZCCS
18. *ner mi*	daughter	D, BD, ZD, CD, BCD, ZCD FZD, FBCD, FZDD, MBDD MZCD, FBCCD, FZSDD FZDCD, MBSDD, MBDCD MZCCD, FFBSCD, FFBDDD FMZSCD, FMZDDD MFBSDD, MMZSDD, MMZDCD, FFBSCCD FFBDSDD, FFBDDCD FMZSCCD, FMZDSDD FMZDDCD, MFBSDCD MMZSSDD, MMZSDCD MMZDCCD	HBD, WBD, HZD, WZD HBCD, WBCD HZCD, WZCD HFBCD, WFBCD HMZCD, WMZCD HFBCCD, WFBCCD HMZCCD, WMZCCD
-x. ——*mi*	——'s son	FFZC, MFZC, FFZCC, MFBDC	
-y. —*ner mi*	——'s daughter	MFZCC, FMBDC, MMBDC FFZCCC, MFBDCC, MFZCCC FMBDCC, MMBDCC FMBSDC, MMBSDC FFZCCCC, FMBDCCC, MFBDCCC MFZCCCC, MMBDCCC FMBSSDC, MMBSSDC FMBSDCC, MMBSDCC	

(continued)

Term	Nearest Designation	Affinal Terms Only
19. *ninge*	husband	H
20. *ner*	wife	W
21. *yamal (bo)*	son-in-law	DH, BDH, ZDH, CDH, BCDH, ZCDH, MBDH FBCDH, FZCDH, MBCDH, MZCDH, FBCCDH FZCCDH, MBCCDH, MZCCDH FFBDDH, FMZDDH, MMZSDH FFBCCDH, FMZCCDH, MMZCCDH FFBCCCDH, FMZCCCDH, MFBSDCDH, MMZCCCDH
	father-in-law	HF, WF, HFF, WFF, HMF, WMF, HFB, WFB, HMB, WMB HBDH, WBDH, HZDH, WZDH, HFZH, WFZH HMZH, WMZH, HFZS, WFZS, FZDH, HMBS, WMBS HFZSS, WFZSS, HMBSS, WMBSS, HBCDH, WBCDH HZCDH, WZCDH, HFZSSS, WFZSSS, HMBSSS, WMBSSS HFBCDH, WFBCDH, HMZCDH, WMZCDH HFBCCDH, WFBCCDH, HMZCCDH, WMZCCDH
22. *yamal ner*	daughter-in-law	SW, BSW, ZSW, CSW, BCSW, ZCSW, FBSW, FZSW FBCSW, FZDSW, MBDSW, MZCSW, FBCCSW, FZDCSW MBDCSW, MZCCSW, FFBSCSW, FFBDDSW, FMZSCSW FMZDDSW, MFBSDSW, MMZSDSW, MMZDCSW FFBSCCSW, FFBDSDSW, FFBDDCSW, FMZSCCSW FMZDSDSW, FMZDDCSW, MFBSDCSW, MMZSSDSW MMZDCCSW
	mother-in-law	HM, WM, HFM, WFM, HMM, WMM, HFZ, WFZ, HMZ WMZ, HFBW, WFBW, HMBW, WMBW, HBSW, WBSW HZSW, WZSW, HFZD, WFZD, HMBD, WMBD, HBCSW WBCSW, HZCSW, WZCSW, HFZSD, WFZSD, HMBSD WMBSD, HFBCSW, WFBCSW, HFZSSD, WFZSSD HMZCSW, WMZCSW, HFBCCSW, WFBCCSW HMBSSD, WMBSSD, HMZCCSW, WMZCCSW
23. *basi (bo)*	sister's husband (female ego)	ZH, FZH, MZH, FBDH, FFBDH, FFBSDH, FMZSDH MMZDDH (not on chart) HB, HSH, HFBS, HMZS
	cousin-in-law (male or female)	FZDH, MBDH, FZSDH, MBSDH, FMZDH, FFBDDH FMZDDH, FZSSDH, MBSSDH, FFBDSDH, FMZDSDH MMZSSDH, MMZSSSDH, FFBDSSDH, FMZDSSDH
24. *basi ner*	sister-in-law	HZ, WZ, BW, WBW, HFBD, WFBD, HMZD, WMZD FBSW, FZSW, MBSW, MZSW, FZSSW, MBSSW, MMBSW FFBCSW, FMZCSW, MFBSSW, MMBSSW MMZCSW, FZSSSW, FFBDSSW, FMZDSSW MFBSSSW, MMBSSSW, MMZSSSW, FFBDSSSW FMZDSSSW, MFBSSSSW, MFBSSDSW, MMBSSSSW
25. *sapu (bo)* *kaplari*	brother-in-law	WZH, HFBDH, WFBDH, HFZDH, WFZDH, HMBDH, WMBDH, HMZDH, WMZDH, HFZDS, WFZDS, HMBDS, WMBDS, HFZDCS, WFZDCS, HMBDCS, WMBDCS MFBSDH, MFBSSDH, MMBSDH, MMBSSDH, MFBSSSDH, MMBSSSDH
26. *sapu ner*	female affine	HFBSW, WFBSW, HMZSW, WMZSW
27. *ka (bo)*	brother-in-law (lit. 'male friend')	WZH, FFZDH, MFZDH, FFZCDH, MFZCDH, FMBDDH MFBDDH, MMBDDH, FFZCCDH, FMBSDDH, FMBDCDH MFBDCDH, MFZCCDH, MMBSSDH, MMBDCDH FFZCCCDH, FMBSSDDH, FMBSDCDH, FMBDCCDH MFBDCCDH, MFZCCCDH, MMBSSSDH, MMBDCCDH

(continued)

Term	Nearest Designation	Affinal Terms Only
		HFZDS, WFZDS, HMBDS, WMBDS, WFBDH HFZDH, WFZDH, HMBDH, WMBDH, WMZDH HFZSDH, WFZSDH, HFZDCS, WFZDCS HFZDDH, WFZDDH, HMBSDH, WMBSDH HMBDCS, WMBDCS, HMBDDH, WMBDDH HFZSSDH, WFZSSDH, HFZDCDH, WFZDCDH HMBSSDH, WMBSSDH, HMBDCDH, WMBDCDH
28. *ka ner*	sister-in-law (lit. 'female friend')	HBW, FFZSW, FMBSW, MFZSW, FFZCSW, FMBDSW MFBDSW, MFZCSW, MMBDSW, FFZCCSW, FMBDCSW FMBSDSW, MFBDCSW, MFZCCSW, MMBSDSW MMBDCSW, FFZCCCSW, FMBSSDSW, FMBSDCSW MFBDCCSW, MFZCCCSW, MMBSDCSW, MMBDCCSW
		HFZSW, WFZSW, HFZDD, WFZDD, HMBSW, WMBSW HMBDD, WMBDD, HFZSSW, WFZSSW, HFZDSW WFZDSW, HFZDCD, WFZDCD, HMBSSW, WMBSSW HMBDSW, WMBDSW, HMBDCD, WMBDCD HFZSSSW, WFZSSSW, HFZDCSW, WFZDCSW HMBSSSW, WMBSSSW, HMBDCSW, WMBDCSW
-a. —*nenge*, —*ner*	——'s spouse (female ego only)	HZH, HFBDH, HMZDH
	(male/female ego)	MBW, MBSW, MBSSW, MBSSSW, FZSSSW FFBW, FFZH, FMBW, FMZH, MFZH MMBW, MMZH, FMBDH, FZSSW, MFBSW, MFBDH MMBDH, MMZSW, FFBDSW, FMBSSW, FMBSDH FMZDSW, MFBSDH, MMBSDH, MMZSSW FFBDSSW, FMBSSSW, FMBSSDH, FMZDSSW MFBSSDH, MMZSSSW, FMBSSSDH, FMZDSSSW FFBDSSSW, FMBSSSSW, MFBSSSSDH, MMZSSSSW

Key to symbols:

F = Father	S = Son	C = Child (either sex)
M = Mother	D = Daughter	P = Parent (either sex)
B = Brother	H = Husband	O = Older
Z = Sister	W = Wife	Y = Younger

Fig. 5. Ketengban kinship terms

Mutual Obligations and Expectations

Kinship terms for the Ketengban are not merely lexical notations for certain slots on a genealogical chart but serve to define the parameters of social interaction between individuals and groups. In some cases these are fairly broad and in others more detailed and, ideally, more binding. In the primary use and in the extension of the terms to one another, people not only keep track of how they are related, but also how they should behave towards one another. Furthermore, these expectations give some basis for evaluation of how well the relationship is being maintained. Poorly maintained relationships have, in the past at least, been grounds for punitive action such as curses (see the first paper of this volume).

Mother's Brother and Sister's Son

As is the case in many of the societies which have been studied in Irian Jaya and Papua New Guinea, the relationship between a man and his maternal uncle (both real and classificatory) is a key one for the Ketengban. Though many of the expectations as well as actual behavior between mother's brother and sister's son are not different in kind from other important dyads such as between brothers or father and son, there is a difference in the degree and frequency of interaction and in the intensity of the personal relationship. One's *mam* 'mother's brother' is a person with whom there is a special bond of intimacy because the *mam* represents one's mother's group or clan in a particular way. Some writers have described this type of relationship as one's "male mother" in that he does for ego significant things that only a male can do, yet he is from the mother's clan. There is not only the fulfilling of a mentor role which is crucial to a person, but there is also a closeness in feeling for one another that resembles the intensity of love between a parent and child. This is evidenced in the usage of the kin terms in that the person referred to as *mam* 'mother's brother' refers back to sister's child as *mi* or *ner mi* 'my child'. The relationship between ego and his mother's brother ties the two clans together economically, socially, and emotionally. This has not only been idealized verbally, but in our observation has been frequently true in behavior.

From early childhood onward, ego's *mam* gives him gifts of food, net bags, prized meat, axes, and other valued goods suitable for exchange. He also offers or may be called upon for help in house building, collecting firewood, opening gardens, and supplying the root stock and seeds for gardens. In periods of difficulty, both during childhood and adult life, one's *mam* is often a key figure in help and support. In sickness he helps procure firewood, food, and water, and attempts to alleviate or cure sickness or injury either directly or by his influence. A *mam* kinsman also supports ego in disputes and fights though this does not seem to be strictly required. If ego (sister's son) brings shame on the clan, the *mam* is often among the key ones reprimanding him in public discussions of the offenses.

Later in life, when a young man is ready to take a wife, his *mam* is frequently considered the best person to select a prospective bride and to arrange the marriage with her parents and relatives. In this role he is called the *ner moromna ngebo* 'the wife-asking man'. Since cross-cousin marriage is preferred, whether actual mother's brother's daughter or classificatory,[4] the *mam* is in a strategic position to exert his influence as 'father' on behalf of his 'child' (in this case a sister's son as groom and perhaps even daughter as bride). He may be the one who acts as mediator of the intricacies of bride price collection and contribute such valued items as pigs, nets, bows, axes, or necklaces. More recently, the bride price might also include newer introductions to the system such as soap, machetes, cloth goods, salt, and money. In the event the *mam* is not the kinsman directly proposing marriage to the bride, he often collects the bride wealth and passes it on to his sister's son and his agnatic kin, who, in turn, relay it through appropriate channels to the kin of the bride.

Although marriages are frequently arranged by the mother's brother, if ego does not marry mother's brother's daughter (perhaps because he already has a wife and does not want another), then ego along with the bride's real brother will have considerable influence in choosing mother's brother's daughter's husband. They will choose another man from among her cross-cousins if possible. Ego is responsible to provide much of the bride price if he is not the groom, thus giving him a strong voice in the matter. If ego does marry his mother's brother's daughter, then mother's brother and his sons will not contribute to the bride price but will receive it. If ego marries some more distant cross-cousin or a woman of a different clan, then the mother's brother and his sons will contribute to the bride price. However, if mother's brother was influential in arranging the marriage, then he will receive some of the bride price but he cannot both contribute and receive bride price during a given exchange.

The *mam* may also help the new family to gain some economic stability and security by opening gardens and providing shoots and seeds for it. If the geographical distance is far enough to preclude much direct help, the *mam* is still expected to participate in key ways in the collection of bride wealth, if on no other occasion.

In fact, if no help is forthcoming on such an occasion, one's *mam* may be verbally disclaimed and the relationship considered broken and shamed. If he eventually does meet the expectations of a good *mam* in this matter,

---

[4]In Omban, a Ketengban village of about four hundred men, women, and children, there are ten to twelve cases of actual mother's brother's daughter marriage, which is about ten percent of the married couples.

the relationship is restored. The Ketengban say that "a good *mam* will always help his sister's son."

The mother's brother and sister's son dyad is a reciprocating relationship and the Ketengban say that all which has just been described of help, support, sharing, and cooperation is mutual. Both the mother's brother and sister's son may request help from each other in need, but usually do not, since both should be careful to notice what the other may be doing or need so as to volunteer support beforehand. Some say it would even be improper to ask for help in times of obvious need, probably not so much a prohibition as a reflection of the clear expectation that well-meaning responsible *mam* kinsmen will always come to one's aid, making the request unnecessary.

Normally, due to obvious age and generational differences, a sister's son is not involved in the major exchanges of bride wealth for his mother's brother. But in larger families, or in the case of classificatory mother's brother where age differences may not be as great, it frequently does happen that a sister's son is involved in helping with some aspects of the bride price collection and distribution for his *mam*.

Although strict obedience is not often required in any Ketengban relationship, in the case of the mother's brother and sister's son dyad, to refuse one's *mam* is to cause a break, not only in the natural authority of elder to younger, but also to break intimacy in a key relationship which is widely nurtured in the society and has ramifications in many spheres of life. One's interaction with mother's brother leads to relationships with a group of kinsmen and provides a balance in the patrilineal society by ties with a network of those in a clan other than one's own. This clan has contributed directly to one's being via conception and birth by one's mother. Often this relationship is marked by a degree of relaxed congeniality and overtly happy friendship that is not commonly seen between a son and his father or his father's brothers, who are all seen as functioning like father, having a parental authority in relationship to him.

Father and Son

As would be expected, the relationship between a father and son in a patrilineal society is fundamental indeed. During the first six or seven years of a child's life, he stays with his mother in her house and then he transfers over to sleeping and staying with his father in the men's house. Thus, until his early teens, a major portion of his acculturation comes via the nuclear family. From his father he learns a great many things about his society and his eventual place in that society as well as his rights and obligations within it. However, a Ketengban boy's acculturation and general education, as well as the modeling of behavior, is also shared by a range of other male kinsmen[5] through association in the men's house from the time he begins sleeping there. But even though a son's circle of models and teachers widens, the Ketengban still feel it is primarily the responsibility of the father to love, care for, and provide for his sons. He is also to teach his sons certain key things, especially those things related to inheritance along patrilineal lines, the essential basic knowledge of gardening and gathering, and matters of proper kin relationships and exchange. In previous times a father handed down clan secrets, spells, and spirit connections to his eldest sons.

A father teaches his sons which of the vast variety of plants, nuts, and fruits in the surrounding jungle are edible and, where it applies, how to plant these and other types of garden produce considered suitable for men to plant.[6] He also teaches his sons where in terms of altitude, proximity to houses, other crops, and water these are to be cultivated for the most efficient results. The skills of house building, fencing, damming streams, and breaking ground for new gardens are taught primarily by a father as his sons play or work alongside him and his male kinsmen or friends in work parties.

The two most important areas of knowledge a son gains from his father are those of inheritance rights and the introduction to important kinsmen, particularly males. A father is careful to show his sons the location of land, springs, and food-bearing plants which he himself has inherited, and to which he has territorial rights to pass on to his sons. He will, for instance, show his sons just where he and his ancestors have planted and still harvest pandanus, bananas, breadfruit, and nuts. He will show his son how to clear the area around this land so that it is apparent to everyone that he recognizes his rights to it and is maintaining and caring for it should anyone else seek to harvest or claim rights to it. This is particularly

---

[5]Among the primary ones are biological and clan brothers, older male cross-cousins (*neiki bo*) and mother's brother (*mam*).

[6]Men commonly plant and transplant from suckers, shoots, or seeds such items as pandanus, taro, bananas, breadfruit, and various kinds of introduced vegetables like tomatoes, soy beans, and peanuts. But they would, for instance, most likely not be involved in planting the new shoots for a sweet potato garden. That is considered more properly the domain of women.

important in that, over time, villages and gardens are relocated to some extent. Also, more recently, where people have gathered in larger heterogeneous villages, garden areas may be farther removed from the houses. These factors mean that a greater number of non-relatives may be traveling through the area or gathering and gardening nearby. Likewise, father teaches his son where *his* own garden and gathering areas are to be and those of others so that he can avoid trespassing in someone else's area. Father also takes his son along as he plants things which will perhaps not produce for years but will be for the son's use. All of these things potentially come to be the possessions of the sons after their father's death or in his very old age, and where disputes arise he has only to argue convincingly that these things are rightfully his on the grounds that his father and grandfathers planted them.

In addition to items which are directly inherited from his father, a son also learns from him who their key relatives are. Many of these kinsmen will form ego's own network of reciprocally sharing kinsmen and have been in such relationship to his father beforehand. It is primarily in this way that a young boy learns who his *mam* and *neiki* kinsmen are and how to relate to them.

A father teaches his son that he needs to be continually visiting and sharing with these kinsmen in order to fulfill his own obligations and to know where his resources are (in terms of material and personnel) in times of need. A son is taught that if he shares the right kinds of things generously, these kin will be eager to help him in return. For instance, if a *mam* kinsman lives far away a piglet is a particularly good gift because it is not only impressive but the kinsman will remember his 'sister's son' as it grows, thus partly overcoming the disadvantage of geographical distance.

Finally, a son receives advice and reprimands from his father in regard to appropriate behavior between the sexes. Among other things, he is counseled not to joke with or be near single women or the wives of other men often, generally to avoid incurring the wrath of their husbands or male relatives, which could result in death or the loss of his inheritance to other kinsmen.

The mother-daughter relationship is similar in teaching and mentoring to that of father-son, especially until the daughter's marriage. After that time this relationship is not a dominant dyad, mostly due to women's general powerlessness in the society and the virilocal residence pattern. For further information on Ketengban women, see the other articles in this volume.

Other Kinsmen

Cross-cousins. neiki mam is the son of ego's *mam*, while *neiki bo* can refer to all other cross-cousins including the sons of *neiki mam* and the sons of other *neiki bo*. However, if ego wants to maintain a close relationship to his mother's brother's family and to teach his children to do the same he will continue to use *neiki mam* for descending generations as well. Thus most of the descriptive information below would apply primarily to *neiki mam* and less strongly to *neiki bo*.

There is a very high degree of similarity between the type of close personal relationship and the kind of help that is reciprocally shared between ego and mother's brother's son (and, reciprocally, father's sister's son, *neiki* kinsmen), as there is between ego and mother's brother. There is the same type of emotional and social bond and a very similar economic relationship. In ways, this relationship can be viewed as a less intense version of the mother's brother and sister's son relationship. Ego and his mother's brother's son share reciprocally in work of all kinds, food and goods exchange, and general support. One obvious difference is that these kinsmen are of the same generation and likelier to be close in age, although with large families and multiple wives the whole range of ages may be represented in both of these relationships. Thus, they are peers (members of separate but interacting clans) who can look forward to the potential of a long and mutually helpful relationship. Because of their age similarity, they often go through the same phases of life together, having the same needs and struggles, and thus taking frequent advantage of the understanding and willingness to help this affords.

In addition, they can potentially be involved in the sister exchange marriage pattern and again contribute to the bonding of two clans in a wide range of interactions. In our observation there is more actual help given between the *neiki* and *mam* kinsmen than any other, and it is the relationship most often talked about.

The relationship of mother's brother to their sister's daughters is similarly parental but of a different nature since the types of help to be expected are totally different. Women have to do primarily with gardens, food preparation, and child care, and since they serve their husband's family, have little opportunity to serve their own *mam* and *neiki mam*.

In-laws. The relationship of male ego to spouse's parents and their clansmen is marked by a certain tension and caution rather than by warm friendship. Since the primary residence pattern is patrilocal, this can be accounted for on the basis of geographical proximity, the wives' relatives often living a considerable distance away. But a significant factor in the tension is that these relatives, if unhappy with the husband, can always demand more bride price. There may never be complete closure of bride wealth payments, leaving the husband and his family always vulnerable. Additionally, there are avoidance taboos related to the wife's ascending generational relatives. Ego may not say the names of his wife's (lineal) grandfathers, her mother's brothers, or her mother. Saying the names of these affines or any word sounding like them is thought to result in insanity, blindness, or loss of teeth, although uttering his wife's actual mother's name is the most dangerous. Physical contact or activities needing physical proximity are also to be avoided. This would include eating food prepared by wife's mother, or using her fire tongs. If ego's affines live nearby, they may make a separate door in the house for ego to use, although Ketengban houses normally have only one door.

Nevertheless, if these affinal kinsmen live close by there may be some degree of friendship and there will probably be fairly frequent visiting and sharing despite the tensions underlying this contact. This visiting seems to center primarily, though not exclusively, around spouse's actual parents. A good relationship will be characterized by occasional help with work projects and minor reciprocal sharing of food. If the older generation *yamal* kin come to visit, they are given food, the use of sleeping mats, and a place to sleep. Upon their departure, usually after one night, if they live close by or within three or four days, ego and his spouse give gifts of some sort. These are not usually large or expensive and may include nets, pandanus, or other foodstuffs. If a man and wife visit the wife's kinsmen, the latter give the gifts to the wife, who later shares them with her husband. If the visit is to the man's kinsmen, the gifts may come directly to the wife (often husband's father to son's wife), or to the son.

A wife's relationship to her affines is more relaxed as she lives near them and serves them. Some Ketengban say she should even use parental kin terms for them. The taboos against proximity to in-laws do not apply to women, although the verbal taboos do.

Thus, the basic pattern seems to be that where *yamal* relations are geographically close, minor sharing, help with work, congenial relations, and visits are encouraged. If a fair distance separates them, these exchanges of visits and help are less frequent and no particular pressure seems to exist to maintain frequent contact.

Siblings. Between male siblings there is a general pattern of mutual help and support throughout life. Brothers help one another with the whole range of daily work and especially with the heavier recurring projects such as house building and opening new gardens. Alternately, if one of the brothers is having friends and kinsmen do a major project for him, the other brothers might help in the collection and preparation of food for the customary feast for the workers at the end of the day or project. Brothers may or may not be part of the same men's house (*bokam* or *nimi ati*), but they will share and visit reciprocally. If the brothers have wives, the demands on their personal energies due to their broadened obligations and commitments to affinal kinsmen—providing for personal security or repaying existing kinsmen obligations incurred in the marriage transaction—may result in less frequent help to siblings. There does seem to be a slight trend towards greater frequency of help to elder siblings than to younger ones. This is, of course, more pronounced when younger siblings are not fully responsible adults. Particularly for males, there is a sense in which the elder has more power and influence at his disposal due to wider contacts and more refined skills. Thus, it is more attractive and eventually more rewarding to help him.

The above is generally true for sisters also. The particulars differ since the division of labor and power in the society are strikingly different for men and women. Brothers will help and receive help from sisters in areas where the culture considers it appropriate. For instance, a brother may help his sister in house building, and a sister may cook to help feed her brother's workers. There is also minor mutual sharing of food stuffs, nets, and other items.

Sisters, while still living together and able to do so, share a special camaraderie and friendship. Together they garden, prepare and collect food, raise pigs and chickens, gather firewood, and participate in the valued and social event of weaving net bags or pig ropes. However, once they marry and move to their husband's homes this closeness diminishes with distance. Therefore, between both same sex and opposite sex siblings, geography may determine or limit the frequency and kind of reciprocal support. It is still considered important to help one another throughout life, and siblings will occasionally come to visit, help, and bring small gifts.

Mental Strategies for Categorizing Kinsmen

During the research for this paper, our Ketengban friends would go through an interesting process to determine what a given individual would be called. In cases where alter had kinship relations with the person questioned, ego could answer readily and usually without hesitation. However, when we were discussing the kinsmen of other people, those involved would work out the appropriate terms by checking through various principles or rules of thumb. These principles gave them the guidelines for the probable best choice of reference. Even when discussing their own kinsmen, wherever confusion or misunderstanding was present on our part, the explanations were given by use of one or more of these principles. Though there does not seem to be a formalized set as regards the exact phrasing, the following statements occurred with great frequency. Since these principles satisfactorily served to clear up questions in the minds of our Ketengban friends when they thought through them in relation to their own or others' kinsmen, it suggests that there is a specific Ketengban strategy or rationale for accurately categorizing kinsmen. Not only were these used by adults to guide their own thinking, but they were also used as teaching aids in explanations to younger speakers and outsiders like ourselves who did not control the system.

Maternal Uncles and Cross-cousins

A *mam* 'mother's brother' must be consanguineally related to ego by a cross-sex distinction (mother to mother's real or classificatory brother), a difference in generation (+1) from ego, and, though not stated explicitly here, an actualization of the relationship by appropriate behavior. This last is important in that failure to fulfill this basis of expected behavior can lead to "disclaiming" a *mam*, or claiming that he is not a very good one. In talking about who may be considered a true *mam*, the most succinct and frequently occurring statement is given in (1), with a closely related and more figurative statement given in (2). With these basic parameters in mind, statement (3) gives the true *neiki* (mother's brother's child) kinsman relationship.

Primary principles:

> (1) "His sister gave birth to me so he is my *mam*."
> (2) "My mother's brother put me on breast milk," or "It was on my mother's brother's breast milk that I grew."
> (3) "All of the children to whom my mother's brothers gave birth are my *neiki* kinsmen."

Extended principles:

> (4) "All of my mother's brothers and the men of her side or clan and generation are my *mam*."
> (5) "I can call my *neiki* [mother's brother's son] kinsmen *mam* [mother's brother] because a woman of their clan gave birth to me."
> (6) "All of the children born to men of my mother's clan or side are my *neiki* kinsmen."
> (7) "Any men who come into our area to live from far away and with whom we have no clan connections, I can call *neiki bo* if we are living close by and sharing and want to live together well."

The *neiki* 'matrilateral cross-cousin' is essentially the same as the *mam* 'mother's brother' relationship except that actualization of the relationship is not so crucial (partly because the expectations are not as major or perhaps as binding), and the generations involved are the same principles (1)–(3).

Since ego is *neiki mam* to his father's sister's children, although he normally calls them his children, he may also reciprocate with *neiki* terms and may call all the classificatory cross-cousins on his father's side by *neiki* 'cross-cousin' terminology. Since the behavioral code is reciprocal, this could be expected, but *neiki* kinsmen are primarily thought to be matrilateral, and the term *neiki mam* is never used of patrilateral kin.

As to the extensional rules (4)–(7), though *mam* may be chosen as the term of reference for mother's clansmen (4), ego may take considerations of generation into account and refer to those who are much older as *apke* 'grandfather' and those of younger ages as *neiki mam* or *neiki bo* 'cross-cousin'. He may also choose to raise the status of alter by calling a cross-cousin *mam* 'mother's brother', even though alter is only slightly older (5). In this case, generation is ignored and ego looks more at all men and women of mother's clan as mother's siblings. The females of the clan are seen as a group of women like mother, and the men as their brothers, although biologically, alter may be mother's brother's son.

The fourth, fifth, and sixth extension principles recognize primarily that alter is in a different clan from ego and that the obligations and expectations of the relationship either have already been realized (as in the past with father), that they are presently being fulfilled, or that a suitable basis for their fulfillment has been established by classifying one another as *neiki*.

The seventh statement recognizes that unless people are to remain uninvolved acquaintances in the same locality, a pattern for which there is almost no traditional basis, they need to give each other kin designations in order to know how to relate properly. A *neiki bo* can be a close kinsman, though without heavy obligations, and must be of a separate clan so it works well as a term for extensions. What makes this fictive *neiki* relationship preferable is that there is a wide range of expectations among different types of *neiki* consanguineal kinsmen, and the extension frees the individuals involved to have as close or distant a relationship as they desire.

Grandfather and Grandmother

Primary principle:

> (1) "The men who gave birth to my father and the men who gave birth to my mother are my grandparents."

Extended principles:

> (2) "The clansmen of the women who gave birth to my mother are my grandkinsmen," or:
> (3) "She is of the women who gave birth to me and is an old woman" [so she is a female grandkinsman].

The primary statement recognizes the crucial direct blood link and the generation ($+2$) difference. In the extension, however, even ego's peers and those who may be slightly younger can and are called grandparent (see figure 2). If, for instance, ego's grandmother was born into clan A and married a man from Clan B, ego, who is of clan C, may then see all clan A members in his lifetime as grandparents by virtue of the grandmother's part in bearing mother. All men of Clan B in mother's generation are called 'mother's brother'.

Consider the case of Elias and Pius diagrammed in figure 6. Pius calls Elias *apke* 'grandfather', and Elias reciprocates with *mi* 'child'. Elias is a Basidoman (B) clan member, and Pius' grandmother was a Basidoman woman. Pius' grandmother's husband was a Diprur (D) man, and so Pius' mother was a Diprur woman. She married a Kulka (K) man and her child, Pius, is a Kulka boy. However, as is outlined above, Pius, remembering that his mother was the offspring of a Basidoman woman, will call all Basidoman clan members 'grandparent'. Elias is only slightly older than Pius but is called 'grandfather'. Likewise, both Manuel, who is an age-mate of Pius, as well as his younger brother who is about eight years younger than Pius, will be called 'grandfather' by Pius because they are Basidoman clan members.

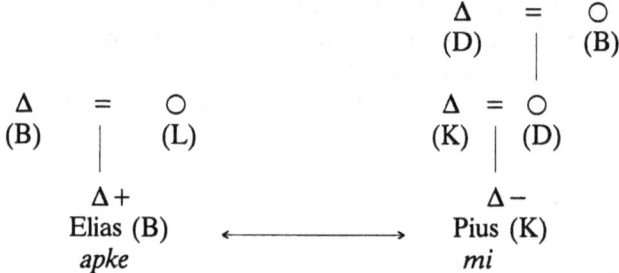

Fig. 6. Grandparent terminology extension

Mother and Father

Ego's biological parents may be designated by stating either of the primary principles below. Father (*nai*) and mother (*nainkon*) may be extended to include the collateral kinsmen of each by the extended statements in (3)–(5). In an extended sense they all "gave birth to me" by virtue of their bloodline from their clan, i.e., mother's clan. Fathers may be extended to those covered by the statement in (6).

Primary principle:

   (1) "He was the one who had intercourse with mother and gave
        being to me."
   (2) "She actually gave birth to me, she is [my body] woman."

Extended principles:

> (3) "All the men of my father's clan are my fathers."
> (4) "All the women of my mother's clan are my mothers."
> (5) "The women of the clan of the woman who gave birth to me are my mothers."
> (6) "He married my mother so I can call him father."

The principles delineating biological parents are straightforward, as are the first two extending principles. In the case of these latter, ego may take into account relative age and choose to call women *nau* 'grandmother', *nanin* 'mother', or *neiki ner* 'cousin'. For male alter, ego may choose to say *apke* 'grandfather' or *nai* 'father'. The fifth statement is simply a restatement of the fourth. In extensions of the sixth type, ego is referring to an affinal link through mother's sisters and other clan women of the parent generation. It can, of course, refer to mother's additional husbands after ego's biological father dies. This includes levirate husbands who are already father to ego, or any other spouse of mother.

Son and Daughter

The following statements are those verbalized regarding use of the terms son (*mi*) and daughter (*ner mi*) in both primary and extended usage.

Primary principle:

> (1) "I had intercourse with my wife and gave being to him/her so he/she is my child."
> (2) "My wife gave being to him/her, so I call him/her my child."
> (3) "I [female speaker] gave being to him/her, so I call him/her child."

Extended principles:

> (4) "Any children born to men of my clan are my children."
> (5) "Any children born to women of my clan are my children."
> (6) "My sibling gave birth to him so he is my child."

The three primary statements simply recognize direct contribution to conception and birth. The extensions in (4) and (5) actually refer to offspring of ego's clan members of ego's generation and descending generations. As seen in earlier sections, elders of ego's clan and ego's mother's clan may be called parents or grandparents to indicate relative age in the terminology. The statement in (6) extends to children of real siblings or parallel cousins in ego's generation.

Siblings

Primary principle:

> (1) "If our fathers and mothers are actually the same persons we are siblings."

Extended principles:

> (2) "If our mothers or fathers are of the same clan we are siblings."
> (3) "Any children born to women of my mother's clan are my siblings."
> (4) "My mother's sister gave birth to him/her so I call him/her sibling."

The specific Ketengban words used in the first statement make it clear that the reference is to a single set of biological parents. The extension in (2) refers to all collateral kinsmen of mother and father in their own generation. The extension in (3) does not explicitly say so, but it always becomes clear in the discussion that the women referred to are women of mother's generation. Statement (4) is essentially the same, simply recognizing that women of mother's clan and age refer to one another as siblings. Sibling terms are used for mother's sister's children as they also are for mother's clan sisters' offspring.

Sister-in-law

The basic principle for using sister-in-law (*basi ner*) is verbalized as:

> "My brother took her as a wife so she is my sister-in-law."

This includes, in Ketengban thinking, the spouses of anyone called brother including all of his clan brothers as well, unless some other consanguineal linkage to that spouse is known. Consanguineal terms would normally supersede the affinal reference.

Brother-in-law

The principles are:

(1) "He took my sister as wife, so he is my brother-in-law."

(2) "If his sister took my brother as husband, he is my brother-in-law."

(3) "My brother's wife's clansmen are my brothers-in-law."

(4) "Their brother took me as wife, so I can call them brother-in-law."

(5) "If our grandkinsmen or fathers traded wives with your clan we can call the men of your clan brother-in-law."

The first two statements can refer specifically to spouses of biological siblings of ego. However, the first three can all be understood in an extended sense by interpreting "sister" in statement one and "brother" in statements two and three as meaning my clan siblings. As worded above, statement two refers to the brothers of ego's brother's spouse. With this particular term, the reader will remember that male ego says *nernye* and female ego says *basi bo*. From the female point of view, statement (4) is used. This refers both to husband's brothers and to his male clan members. The fact that men of spouse's generation are in view is implied. A much broader extension of this particular term is given in (5). This usually seems to be in reference to men of ego's generation, and means that our clan gave women to your clan. It is likely that the reverse situation would still allow for this extension.

Parent-in-law

For parent-in-law (*yamal bo, yamal ner*) it is said:

(1) "My wife's father and mother and their clan people are my parents-in-law."

(2) "My daughter's husband and all his fathers and mothers and their clan people are my *yamal* kinsmen."

The "clan people" to whom reference is made are not people in ego's generation, but are ego's parents' peers and those in other ascending generations.

Extensions of Kin Terms

It is clear as one lives among members of a society like the Ketengban that in daily interaction with close friends and kinsmen, and in certain special cases, people do not always use kin terms in a rigid fashion. Though there are clearly primary sets of kinsmen to whom each term applies which can be thought of as the core or basic relationships thereby delineated, this is not the total picture. While it is true that some terms are much more restricted in usage than others, thinking of kin terms as defining a prescribed group beyond which terms cannot be extended does not account for what actually takes place as people interact. The following section is a brief discussion of some common extensions in Ketengban kin terminology. What is clear is that not only are the terms and categories marked, but also the way they are used and extended in the system is reflective of the kinds of interaction among the Ketengban. As others have pointed out, "the interaction which establishes a relationship may determine the term which should be used" (Shaw 1974:13). Conversely, to some degree the fact of commonly understood and shared roles and expectations for given relationships (marked by certain terms) means that using certain terms can strongly influence the direction a relationship will take or the tone of that relationship in the future. Again, similar to the observations Shaw reports for the Samo of Papua New Guinea, geographical location and place of residence are influential for the Ketengban both in the application of some terms and the degree of fulfillment of the roles implicit in them.

Parent-child

As a means of showing respect and deference, and as a means of expressing a general sense of group unity, the kin terms of the parent and child generations are commonly extended. Thus, any man or woman who is enough older than ego to be considered of comparable age to ego's parents may be politely, respectfully referred to and addressed as *nai* 'father' or *nainkon* 'mother', respectively. (For terms of address and reference see figure 3.)

These people would then reciprocate using the terms *mi* 'male child' or *ner mi* 'female child'. In this case clan and other actual kin connections are not in view; if they exist and, especially, if they are close they would supersede this usage. These terms could be used for an older adult or child from any location or clan. As used here, there are no real expectations of reciprocation or other special behavior. But politeness, the courtesy of deference to elders, and recognition of the dependence of children are generally expected. The younger person is not expected to actually obey or follow the advice of the elder, but neither is the elder expected to care for the younger. What is in focus is proper etiquette—an expression of respect or a recognition of the elder's influence and power.

This focal point is in striking contrast to the primary application of these terms to parallel kinsmen of the parent generation and their spouses. They are emically considered as parents, and there are definite obligations and expectations, just as for biological parents. Similarly, the clan members of father and mother, although one step removed from biological parents and their same-sex siblings, are still considered "closer" in terms of potential obligations and relationships than the general populace to which I am now referring. However, where there is close proximity of housing and living space, together with ongoing congenial interactions, people may actually behave towards one another and regard one another as parent and child. Where relations are not particularly good and no real interest in developing them exists, people may simply refer to one another as *wisi ning* or *wisi nerepe* 'older men' or 'older women', *nyape* or *ner nyape* 'male children' or 'female children'.

Unrelated Peers

Similarly, peers who have no actual clan or genealogical connection may call one another *kap* or *kau* 'friend'.[7] This term may have a range of meaning in terms of actual behavior depending on the degree of personal closeness. What we are referring to here is its usage as a polite "no-strings-or-responsibilities-attached" term of respect between generational peers. In this sense, it may also be used to refer to people who have come from distant areas to live in ego's home area. Of course, kin or nonkinsmen may refer to one another reciprocally and informally as *kau* 'friend'. This application of the term is mentioned again in the final section on priorities.

---

[7]For male friends, *kap* or *ka bo*; for female friends, *ka ner*; for ego of either sex *kau* when referring to a friend of either sex.

Cross-cousins

As reported throughout Melanesia, extension of kin terms is common in the case of outsiders coming to live in ego's area. Since there are no known clan or clear genealogical connections to such a person, he falls into a general category of "others." As explained above, ego may wish to let the situation remain so and simply refer to him as *kap* 'friend', or *nun nimi* 'our men', meaning not much more than 'someone who is of our language and race'. However, if relations between the newcomer and ego are good and both parties are interested in close relations and are likely to "live together well," ego may begin referring to the newcomer as *neiki* 'cross-cousin' kinsman. That is, the newcomer is someone of a clan other than ego's, but with whom ego can have a close personal relationship, and who, more significantly, having now been made a cross-cousin, can be considered as the source of marriage partners. This opens a whole new network of potential reciprocal relationships. This particular extension of terms tends to draw people together, allowing them to see and behave towards one another as kinsmen with a history, though fictive, of mutual aid and support and an expectation of a future of mutually beneficial interactions. This has potential for personal benefit, but also contributes greatly to group solidarity, serving to ameliorate some of the possible intra-group friction and tensions. It is noteworthy, in contrast, that the term *mam* 'mother's brother' which carries associations of greater expectations, is not extended in this way.

The advantages of this broadening of *neiki* terminology for the present day Ketengban culture are considerable. As has been pointed out, now much more than in the past, there is a trend towards larger, centralized, and more heterogeneous villages. Additionally, there is increasing population and greater travel. Both of these factors bring people into daily contact who might otherwise have lived in smaller, more exclusive hamlets.

The *neiki* 'cross-cousin' term may also be applied by a male ego to his brother's wife. The usual term used in reference to brother's wife is *basi ner*, but because it extends further to the female siblings of brother's wife who are potential marriage partners for ego, it is less desirable because it implies no consanguineal relationship when a cross-cousin marriage is preferred. The female siblings of brother's wife, because of the historical practice of levirate marriage and the ideal of cross-cousin marriage, are potential marriage partners for male ego. Ego's mother's brother's daughter could therefore be both cross-cousin and brother's wife. Also, sister exchange, of both biological and clan sisters, has been and still is an attractive marriage option.[8] It is said that, if a man's relationship is good with his brother and brother's spouse, then it is good to refer to brother's wife as *neiki ner*, even if she is not of mother's clan, that is, not actually mother's brother's daughter. She is moving into something of a closer relationship with ego by a consanguineal connection and is being included as a member of mother's clan, to which there are important ties and into which ego should marry.

In cases where brother's wife is in fact a cross-cousin, she would not be referred to as *basi ner*. This would be considered impolite in that it ignores the prior genealogical link and the crucial importance of the network of people the *neiki* relation represents and the closeness they are expected to have with one another. Where there is no connection to mother's clan and thus no expectations of reciprocity, *basi ner* is the acceptable term. An actual mother's brother's daughter or woman of the mother's clan is spoken of as being "from my mother's side (clan or area) woman." A frequently verbalized key reason for preferring a wife who is mother's brother's daughter is that "she will listen to what I say, obey well and work well." The implication is, partly, that since mother was a good worker and provider who loved ego, girls of that clan will be of the same stock and character via mother's brother (*mam*) and will be as good a woman as mother was. On the other hand, it is said that if she is not of mother's clan there is no particular compulsion for her to behave this way and she may or may not "behave properly." It is not uncommon to hear the wife ask rhetorically in domestic quarrels between partners of this type, "Did our mothers give birth to you?" as a reason for not following a husband's orders. To restate the point: referring to one's brother's wife as *neiki ner* and not simply *basi ner* is a way of expressing the acknowledgement of or the expectation and hope for a closer relationship. It elevates both the status and value of the relationship.

---

[8]Many aspects of the whole sphere of marriage have changed dramatically among the Ketengban in the last decade, but greater detail as to marriage practice and custom and the effects and patterns of change are beyond the scope of the present paper. Suffice it to say that, although sister exchange is still an attractive option for marriage, the conditions under which it is arranged for and carried out have changed considerably. In addition, though some men now have multiple wives and others continue to marry additional wives, the practice of polygyny appears to be rapidly decreasing.

As Elder, So Younger

Another type of strategy for referring to people for whom it may be unclear just what, if any, actual connection exists, is to use terms which correspond to the ones used by one's father. One very important way in which this is realized is when there has been a longstanding relationship between one's father or grandfather and another individual. For instance, whether or not a clear genealogical connection can be worked out if father traded with and related to alter as he might to a *mam* 'mother's brother' kinsmen, ego would then relate and refer to him in the same way. This would be true with whatever the relationship was said to be and could even be extended to the members of the same clan as the individual with whom there was a relationship in the past. We have been told numerous times that, "Well, we don't know what the genealogical connection is, but father reciprocated with him (or his clan) as to a mother's brother, so we do also."

Priorities of Terminology

There does seem to be a kind of hierarchy of terminology in cases in which ego could legitimately refer to alter by one of two or more kinship terms. For instance: the same Elias of the Basidoman clan (B) mentioned previously took as a wife the biological sister of a man who is very near his own age (see figure 7). Therefore, this man Ales is wife's brother or *nernye* 'brother-in-law' to Elias. However, Ales is of the Lepitalen clan (L) and Elias' mother was a Lepitalen woman. It is considered that Ales' clan mother gave birth to Elias, so Elias should call Ales *mam* 'mother's brother' rather than *nernye* because the former is a closer and more powerful relationship. Ales, then, can call Elias *mi* 'child' or *neiki mam* 'matrilateral cross-cousin'.

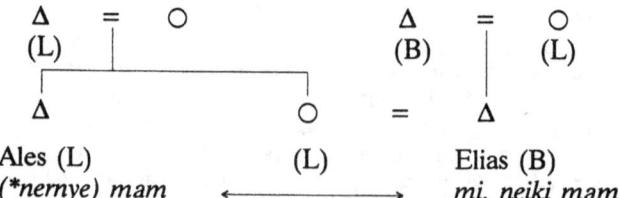

Fig. 7. Illustration of terminology hierarchy 2

Similarly, a man named Obes took a wife from the Kulka clan (K) who is brother's daughter to a man named Musah (see figure 8). Musah refers to this girl as *ner mi* 'female child'. Therefore, Obes has married Musah's daughter and is daughter's husband to Musah or *yamal bo* 'son-in-law'. The term is reciprocal so Obes can call Musah *yamal bo* 'father-in-law'. However, Obes' mother was Kulka and considered sister to Musah who is, therefore, *mam* 'mother's brother' to Obes. Obes must call Musah *mam* 'mother's brother' and not *yamal*.

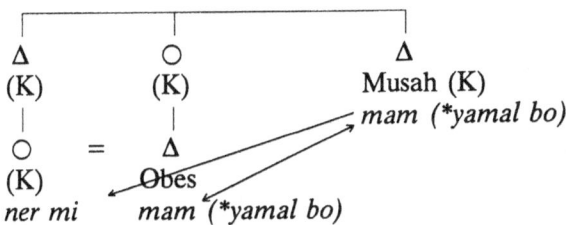

Fig. 8. Illustration of terminology hierarchy 3

In both the above cases there is a superseding consanguineal connection that suppresses the use of the affinal term, a kin relation in which there is not necessarily a strong personal or reciprocating expectation. One's *yamal* and *nernye* relations are often outsiders in terms of bonds between clans. Consanguineal terms supersede affinal terms and preference is also often given to the highest generational term appropriate if there are good relations. So, for example, if ego could appropriately call a certain woman *nainkon* 'mother' but generational factors would allow for it at all, he might very likely call her *nau* 'grandmother'.

This same factor is illustrated by the example of Amos and Semuel (see figure 9). Amos is of the Kulka clan and his mother was a Lepitalen woman, so men of the Lepitalen clan like Semuel, who are of the same generation as Amos, would be called his *neiki bo* kinsmen, as they are mother's brothers' sons to Amos. However, as Semuel is slightly older than Amos, and it is considered a raise in status and respect to do so, Amos can and often does refer to Semuel as *mam* 'mother's brother'.

$$\begin{array}{ccc} \triangle & = & \bigcirc \\ \text{(K)} & \big| & \text{(L)} \\ & \big| & \\ & \triangle - & \end{array}$$

Amos (K)
neiki bo ⟵⟶ *neiki bo, mam*

$$\begin{array}{ccc} \triangle & = & \bigcirc \\ \text{(L)} & \big| & \\ & \big| & \\ & \triangle + & \end{array}$$

Semuel (L)

Note: If Semuel were younger than Amos, Amos would call Semuel *mam* or *neiki mam*.

Fig. 9. Illustration of terminology hierarchy 4

The principle that the closest blood link term is preferred may again be illustrated by the example of Amos Kulka and a man called Nas (see figure 10). Amos is a Kulka man and his mother was a Lepitalen woman. Therefore, Lepitalen men of his generation are his *neiki bo* kinsmen cross-cousins. Nas is the son of a Lepitalen man, but his mother is a Kulka woman of the same generation as Amos and therefore his classificatory sister. Thus, Nas is sister's son to Amos who refers to Nas as *mi* 'child'. Nas reciprocates with *mam* 'mother's brother'. This is considered preferable even though from the first point of view they could have referred reciprocally to one another as *neiki bo* 'cross-cousin'.

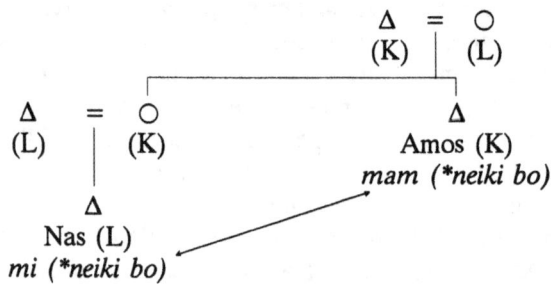

Fig. 10. Continuation of terminology hierarchy 4

A very similar pattern is commonly observed which has the effect, in certain circumstances, of "equalizing" kinsmen who may actually be in a clearly hierarchical relationship genealogically. For instance, it is very common for both men and women to refer to one another as *kau* 'friend'. A context in which this is appropriate is during a work project or the discussion of current issues, or simply in chit-chat. Male kinsmen frequently do this during discussion of some topic which may be highly emotive and potentially dividing. It is generally initiated by the one holding higher status. Thus a *mam* or *apke* may refer to his *mi* 'sister's son' as *kau* in this way. Even wives may refer to husbands as *ka bo* or husbands to their wives as *ka ner* as a means of showing that the relationship is in good condition, and there is enough positive feeling so that using the terms *ninge* 'husband' or *ner* 'wife' seems unnecessary or even slightly distant. This is said to be a "soft" or "pleasant" way of speaking.

Summary

In discussion of expectations and obligations for some of the kinship relationships, the observer notes that not only are there definite cultural expectations for some key kin relations, but also the extension of these terms outside their primary ranges is one means of setting up hopes and expectations that strongly influence the type of personal interactions between people, whether kinsmen or other. Mother's brother's relationship with sister's son emerges as a key to a whole network of wider social and economic relations characterized by interdependency and reciprocating support.

Appendix 1: Verbalized Nuances in Key Relationships

Person	Ketengban Terms	English Description
Pairs:		
husband-wife	*sun ninge butini*	those two people
any close dyad	*sun kange kwirye kupke*	their minds/happiness is straight (one)
	kange tenpu, ninge butini	two people with one mind/happiness
brother-sister	*sun weitap duap*	siblings
brother-brother	*weite du*	siblings
sister-sister	*weitapselip*	siblings
sister-sister	*weit ner, du ner*	older/younger sister
Individuals:		
female playmates	*uruna nerepe*	females who come to play/visit
polygynist	*ner isamka ngop*	a person rich in wives
	ner butini ngop	a two-wife person
age mates	*amse nenge*	people (men) who are together,
	kikiman nenge	or the same
widow, widower	*soli ner, soli ngop*	widow woman, widower man
levirate wife	*soli ner*	
ancestors	*-oupo neng/yape*	language men/people
	-apu neng	grandfather men
	-apke neng	grandfather men
	co puna neng	rotten wood men
	co deiyo neng	the people at the tree base
	yal kemna neng	the people who made/did the shoots (root stock) for the clan
a common ancestor	*tenpu ngop gereksua ngop*	one person that tied us together
bachelor (not yet married youth)	*kaper ngop/ner*	a light (weight) man/woman, or a carefree person
spinster (not yet married girl)	*kanam ngop/ner*	

(continued)

Person	Ketengban Terms	English Description
first child	*dunge*	the oldest
	menmenange	the first
	weni mi/wenye	eldest
middle child	*tarumna mi/ner mi*	additional child
second wives (other than levirate)	*tarumna ner*	additional wife
last child	*siria mi/ner mi/siriange*	the end or outer edge child
	kale mi/ner mi/kalenge	
offspring	*sun nyapselip*	their children
	nun di deiringe nyape	the ones we "put"
illicit child	*yut mi/ner mi*	illicit intercourse
	nyang kolongne mi/ner mi	child
adopted child	*gwanamne mi*	cared for child
friend	*kap/kau/ka/kapu (plus sex)*	friend
	ai ngop/nenge	
namesake	*atem ngop*	namesake man
enemy	*yu (mutu) ngop*	a hostile-area person
	posunung nenge	people who kill us
stranger	*mendiramep neng*	people we don't see
	yuk mutu neng	people of another area
barren woman	*you nere*	barren woman
childless or single person	*taren nere/ngop*	so far single or
	kanam nere/ngop	childless woman or
	kaper ner/ngop	man
woman with one child	*mi/gau deiprop nere*	woman who puts (child)
woman with children	*nyape deiprop nere*	potatoes (food gatherer)
levirate polygynist	*soli ner dopu ngop*	a man who took a widow
	soli ner daku ngop	a man who picked a widow
orphan	*lyan mi/ner mi*	orphan boy/girl
	wein mi	
youngest siblings of parent	*nai/nin kalye*	end/last father/mother

Appendix 2: Alternate Kin Terms

Kinsman	Alternate Terms
grandfather	*-apu bo*
	-apke
	-oupu bo
man	*bo*
	ngebo
	ngop
mother	*nainkon*
	nanin
	nin
	nonge nerepe
friend	*kau*
	kai/kae
	ka (bo), ka ner
	-ai nenge (pl)
male friend of female	*nakinge*
sister	*ka ner*
polygynist	*soli ner daku ngop*
	soli ner dopu ngop
	ner botini ngop
	ner isamka ngop
single female	*taren ner*
	kaper ner
	kanam ner
age mates	*amse nenge/nerepe*
	kikiman nenge/nerepe
ancestors	*co puna yape/nenge*
	co deiyo yape/nenge
	yal kemna yape/ nenge
	yal deiyo yape/nenge
last child	*siriange/siria mi/ner mi*
	kalenge /kale mi/ner mi

References

Lounsbury, Floyd G. 1964. The structural analysis of kinship semantics. In Horace G. Lunt (ed.), Proceedings of the Ninth International Congress of Linguistics, 1073–93. The Hague: Mouton.

Peckham, Nancy. 1981. "My elders, my helpers" Mairasi kinship and marriage. Irian 9(3):43–65.

Shaw, R. Daniel. 1974. Kinship studies in Papua New Guinea. Ukarumpa, Papua New Guinea: The Summer Institute of Linguistics.

Sims, Andrew and Anne. 1981. Ketengban phonology. In Marit Kana (ed.), Workpapers in Indonesian Linguistics 1:50–74. Jayapura: Universitas Cenderawasih in cooperation with The Summer Institute of Linguistics.